Escape from the Little White Crosses

Hellyn Lackey Jordan

ESCAPE from the
Little White Crosses

Stories of World War II from the Front Lines to the Home Front

Hellyn Lackey Jordan

ESCAPE from the Little White Crosses

Copyright © 2000
by
Hellyn Lackey Jordan

First Printing, 2000
Second Printing, 2000

Cover Art by H.L.J.

ISBN 0-9704474-0-X

Published by H. L. Jordan
318 James Ave.
Ashburn, GA 31714
(229) 567-2507

Published in the United States by
Morris Publishing
3212 East Highway 30
Kearney, NE 68847
1-800-650-7888

Dedication

To the children and grandchildren of the men and women whose stories are told here. May you some day realize they did this for you.

CONTENTS

ACKNOWLEDGMENTS

Although this book is rather small, it has consumed an enormous chunk of my time over the past several months. I could never be a Tolstoy or a Margaret Mitchell, writing those enormous volumes!

Through it all, my patient husband has *remained* patient. I thank him for that, and I thank him for his contribution toward making it possible for me to live in a free country, even before he knew me.

To record these stories, I have made several out-of-town trips, made long distance telephone calls galore, or interviewed these people in my home. Let me say thanks to Gene and Bill Cheatham, Joe Simmons, Bill Camp, Fred Wiley, and John Jordan for their brave and heroic deeds. They have all argued with me on that point, but I remain relentless. And, adding Mary Cheatham and Billie Caldwell to the list, I want to thank all of them for being willing to share their stories, and for working with me on the telephone, face to face, and through the mail so that the facts would be facts.

The student interviews in chapters 11 and 12 shed a lot of light on the way civilian lives were affected at that time. I appreciate these stories also, and the adults who gave their time to those students.

I don't profess to be a skilled writer, so I have had to write and re-write, edit and re-edit, and write it again so many times I can almost hear my computer crying, "Gimme a break!" So, I also want to thank all who read this only for its stories, and not to critique its literary style.

INTRODUCTION

These short stories were told to me by men whose lives were spared, some very narrowly, during World War II. Brothers, cousins, or friends may have been left beneath one of the hundreds of thousands of little white crosses lined up row upon row on foreign soil. Some of the men wondered aloud as we talked, "Why did I escape when my buddies were falling all around me?"

Before I began work on these stories, I vowed to make every word and every sentence as accurate as possible. One wrong statement, date or place would invalidate the entire book in the mind of a reader who might have been there.

We tend to make heroes of our deceased loved ones by either exaggerating or misquoting their deeds, however unintentionally. Because of that, only stories of the living, those to whom I could talk with personally, have been included here.

First, I recorded their words on tape as I sat and conversed with them. I had lots of questions for each one, which prompted them to talk more. One of the men said he was telling me things he had not talked about in more than 50 years. He admitted it had been good therapy.

Secondly, there was the task of changing each interview from a conversation into story form. Determined to be absolutely sure that I had not misconstrued any facts during that transition, or failed to convey their thoughts clearly, a copy of the chapter containing their biography was then sent to each person for correction or reproof.

Several friends and relatives, hearing of my endeavor, have wanted their husband's or brother's story included. I realize that I do have other family members with great stories that could have been included, but I had to draw a line somewhere. I drew that line by writing only World War II stories of my husband, brothers, and brothers-in-law.

"Must have been a biiiig family!" you're thinking. Well, yes. My parents died when my siblings and I were very young, and our father's sister became our legal guardian. She brought up her own children, who were our cousins, and four of us just as if we were one big family of brothers and sisters. I still consider them so.

I did make an exception in my writings and branched out to another cousin when telling about women in defense, but the war experiences of those in the military came only from my 'brother-cousins,' brothers-in-law, and of course, my husband. Let me introduce them to you:

Aunt Maude Cheatham, my dad's younger sister, had two sons whose stories are told here. Bill is the older one and saw action in the Pacific. Gene served in Europe, and it was his story that prompted this writing. As a young single lady, Bill's wife Mary worked in a defense plant making ammunition.

Billie Rogers Caldwell, who helped build B-29 bombers, is the daughter of my dad's other sister. She insists she was not the inspiration for the well-known "Rosie the Riveter" featured on the war-time posters seen everywhere, designed to encourage women to go to work in defense plants.

My oldest sister, Mary Nell, is married to Bill Camp, and Dorothy (Dot), my next sister, is married to Joe Simmons.

Fred Wiley is married to my husband's sister. And last, but certainly not least, is my own husband, John Jordan.

I hope you have enjoyed meeting my family and will learn something from reading their stories. I also hope you will always remember what they did for all of us.

PART ONE

Why Another Book About World War II?

❖ CHAPTER 1

Why Another Book About World War II?

At a Veterans Day ceremony recently, a child about eight years of age was heard asking, "Dad, what is a veteran?" Referring to the military, the dictionary says a veteran is *one who has had service or experience in warfare.* It doesn't mention what age or gender one must be to qualify. Some might think of silver-haired old men who need a cane for assistance, but I have seen maimed young men who were war veterans at 20 years old. Some of them are now those silver-haired old men with canes.

These stories are not intended for any purpose other than to record the experiences of my closest family members who are veterans of World War II, and hopefully to show younger generations how all Americans rallied together to win that horrific war.

Jobs left vacant by the draft, and jobs created by war industries had to be filled. Older people came out of retirement, the handicapped did whatever they could, and women by the hundreds of thousands left their comfortable lifestyles to help fill these vacancies.

Included are the stories of two of these women from my own family who worked in a munitions plant and an airplane factory. I consider these women 'veterans' too, in a sense. They definitely helped to win that war.

I am a retired teacher who taught social studies in a middle school. Now, if you are of an older generation like myself, you might never have heard of a subject called social studies. In our day it was called "hist'ry and joggerphy." This is an important subject that regrettably gets too little attention in most of our present-day schools.

My 6th grade history book covered the Middle East, Europe, and Africa. The students just loved ancient Egypt with its mummies and pyramids. Later, they decided that the Middle Ages unit with its knights and castles was even more fun. But when we came to the unit on World War I and World War II, they had the idea that this would be just another boring war to study about. I am thankful to say that their summaries at the end of the year showed that WW I and II had become the favorite unit for more than half the students.

I told my classes that there are many people still living today, people they may know, who made this chapter in history. When I announced that one of their assignments would be to interview someone who was living during World War II, almost without exception someone in the class would say, "I don't know anybody that old!" It was hilarious to hear the children gasp when I told them that *I was living during WW II!* I was just a child about their age, and grew into a young teenager during WW II, and my own father was a survivor of poison gas during WW I. Their young minds could not imagine it. But one of the greatest things that came from these interviews was that so many of the children learned for the very first time that Grandpa, or Uncle Bud, or a neighbor was a veteran of WW II.

The number of veterans of those wars is diminishing rapidly as we enter a new century. The classroom teachers who can tell their students about personal experiences from that era will all be retired soon. I can only hope that the students who were in my classes will pass down the stories they heard. They will surely not forget the POW who came to speak to them about the treatment he was forced to endure by the enemy during his capture and imprisonment. Nor will they forget the 'museum' we created in our classroom with mementoes loaned to us by grandparents, uncles, or neighbors who dug into their dusty attic trunks or treasure boxes when a child asked for an interview about WW II. The room was filled with photographs, censored letters, ration books, old uniforms, fringed satin pillow covers painted with poems to 'Mother', 'Sweetheart', 'Wife', or 'Sister'. There were medals and ribbons, and even a gold star on a banner that had hung in a window to signify that someone from that home would not be coming back.   There was a folded American flag that once had draped a casket, and souvenirs of all kinds were brought from homes across the county.

Only in recent years do I remember veterans talking so freely about their experiences.   Could it be that they are heartbroken when they see the growing disrespect for our flag, a symbol of the freedom they risked their lives to keep? Could it be that they want to yank every baseball cap from every head in the ball park when the national anthem is being sung? Could it be that they see our nation losing its sense of patriotism?   Or could it be that those of us who care are encouraging them to talk as we realize that it may too soon be too late?

Recently, I was listening to the harrowing WW II experiences of one of these veterans, and about his trip back to Europe a few years ago to try to locate the family in Belgium who had saved his life. I already knew parts of the story because he is my brother --- well, almost. His mother was my father's sister, and she took me into her home after my siblings and I were orphaned in 1941. How well I remember the anguish of my aunt when two sons had to leave for war, and then when this one came home in agony and unable to walk. But that story later.

Listening to his story, I told him that he should put all of that in writing. Our children and grandchildren need to know that WW II was fought and won by people we know and love. It is not just another chapter in a history book that records dates, or points out places on a map.

Then I thought about the other cousin who was as close as a brother. He was serving our country in the Pacific at the same time, and he also had a story to tell. Their mother kept a map of the world hanging on the wall beside the radio in the dining room where the family gathered. We might call it the family room today. As the war news was broadcast over the radio and we heard about certain armies pushing through, or being pushed back, she would stick a pin in the place on the map and say, "That's where my boy is." Then she would say a prayer for him. Scenes like that made an indelible impression even on a young child.

I used to tell my classes that any man or woman who put on a uniform, knowing that they might be required to risk their life for us, was a hero in my sight. I have been married to one of those heroes since 1948.

I met my husband when I was 17 years old and he was 21. At that young age, he was already a veteran of the war in Europe. Then the thought struck me, "Here are three men, two 'brothers' and my own husband. How much closer can you get to some great stories that need to be recorded for our descendants!" So, armed with a tape recorder, I began my quest to get the stories I have transcribed on these pages.

There is no way that I could relate the experiences of everyone I know – or have known – because there was probably no American family living at that time who was not affected by the war, so I have chosen the stories of those closest to me, and whom I can interview personally. Already I have missed the opportunity to talk to some very close family members. My husband's brother, Lt. Commander Ray Jordan died in 1978. He was a career Navy veteran and at the time of his retirement was hospital administrator in Yokohama, Japan. Another of his brothers, Chester Jordan, who served with the Army's Signal Radio Intelligence Company in Europe, died in 1999. My oldest sister's first husband, Tom Evans, lost his life to cancer several years ago, but I am told that he served in a high security capacity during the testing of the atomic bomb, and that he actually assisted in loading the bomb onto the *Enola Gay*, the airplane that dropped the first of these bombs on Japan. Other close relatives have served in subsequent wars such as Korea, Viet Nam, and the Gulf War. Still others have served during peace time, including my own son Mark who served in the U.S. Navy for six years. I will limit my writings to WW II.

Following the biographies are some insights into life as a civilian at that time, and how even young children had a part in the war effort. I have included these to emphasize how war affects *everyone*. War is not the glorified action played by actors on a television or movie screen. It is real people spilling real blood, and leaving heartbreaking voids in the lives of people who loved them. It is about handsome, fuzzy-faced eighteen and nineteen year olds lo.... a limb or an eye or a life. It is about live-or-die situations that create such unimaginable fear in a man that his life is ruined forever.

May God bless America, and grant peace to the world.

PART TWO

European Theater of Operations

❖ CHAPTER 2

John D. Jordan

This first biography is that of the most important man in my life, my husband, with whom I have shared my life since I was just a young girl only 18 years old. He had not been discharged from military service but a few months when I met him in 1947, and I thought he was the skinniest man I had ever seen! After being home for several months and eating his mom's good cooking, he began to "fill out," as country folks say, and look normal. We were married in July of 1948 but I still didn't know the full story of his experiences for many years. After more than 50 years, he has agreed to share them.

John Durwood Jordan was born in September of 1925 in Laurens County, Georgia. His father was a railroad telegrapher and, coached by his dad, John learned Morse code at a very early age by hanging around the depot much of his life. During high school he worked as a station laborer, doing some clerical work and learning the workings of a railroad depot.

After thousands upon thousands of young men had to leave their homes and jobs for military service, the railroads were in grave need of personnel. Moving troops and supplies was critical, and so was the need for someone to keep the railroads in operation. So Southern Railway, having known John through his father, and from his working in and around a depot much of his life, began to pursue this young man for employment. He was still too young to enter military service during the early years of the war.

In 1943, he stood the test and was hired *by mail* because of the immediate need for telegraph operators, which was the only way to move trains in those days. He was sent to Pinehurst,

Georgia on his first job in September, just shy of his 18th birthday. He stayed there only about 30 days and was sent to Sycamore, Georgia as station agent. By this time he had turned 18 and the process of induction into the military had begun.

The ordeal of all draftees involved reporting to the place of registration, which in John's case was Valdosta because he was then a resident of Lowndes County. There the young men were loaded onto buses and transported to Fort McPherson near Atlanta for physical examinations. This took three days out of John's job, which posed a problem for both the railroad and himself. Two days were spent in traveling there and back, and one day for the exams. Due to a lazy-eye problem that had caused poor vision in his left eye since childhood, he was classified as 1-A, limited service, and sent back home to wait.

This ordeal was repeated every month until March when this otherwise healthy young man was fed up with the wasted time and inconveniences. This time, with the same results and the same classification being given to him, he asked to see the recruiting officer to volunteer. He was accepted and requested railroad operations. Fortunately, he was assigned to the 734th Railway Operating Battalion that was forming in New Orleans. At last he was in the United States Army. It was 1944.

So off he went to New Orleans where he spent bivouac in a pup tent during a monsoon. After basic training there, he was sent to Van Buren, Arkansas, for technical training. He worked as a telegraph instructor there, later being sent to Wagoner, Oklahoma for a few weeks of railroad experience.

Following a brief furlough home, he was sent to Camp Kilmer, New Jersey, in November and loaded onto a liberty ship to be sent to Europe. Liberty ships were ships that were hastily built for transporting troops and supplies. They were welded together to save construction time rather than being riveted.

John's ship was part of a large convoy which, as all others crossing the Atlantic Ocean at that time, was in grave danger of enemy submarines. The crossing took 15 grueling days, including Thanksgiving Day, 1944.

Landing at Liverpool, England, the troops were taken to a camp at Darby-On-Trent for almost two weeks before moving to

Southampton for the channel crossing to the European mainland. I can't be sure that his next statement isn't slightly exaggerated, but I quote him as saying that they ate Brussels sprouts for breakfast, dinner, and supper for the entire two weeks. I DO know that I don't dare put Brussels sprouts on the table and expect him to eat them, even after more than 50 years.

At Southampton, they were loaded onto an English troop ship and moved by night to Port of LeHavre in northern France. The port had been destroyed by bombing, so the troops went ashore in LSTs. From there they marched eight miles out into the French countryside and, as John puts it with his ability to paint a word picture in few words, "We set up camp in a mud puddle, and slept in that puddle for several nights."

The next phase was their first encounter with European railroads. The men were loaded onto cattle cars that were called 40-and-eights. They got their name because they could hold 40 men or eight horses, so he tells me. Two or three men could stretch out in the car while the others stood or sat. This was endured for four days and four nights while they crossed France and Belgium, stopping just long enough for field rations provided by the kitchen car on the train.

I asked him about their warmth during that trip, having read about the severe Decembers in parts of Europe. In his slow Southern accent he explained, "We were GIs, so we were not so concerned about the cold, or whether we could sit or lie down. We just had to get where we were going and get the job done."

They arrived at Maastricht in the Netherlands on Christmas Eve of 1944 and occupied the loft of the enormous railroad passenger station. Even though they were on a hard board floor, they could at least stretch out. The greatest luxury was a hot bath, which they had not had in more than a month. I wondered at the fact they didn't have fungus or lice. John said solemnly, "Lice wouldn't have had anything to do with us."

To 'celebrate' Christmas Day, John's group was sent to the next post at Heerlen, a coal mining town also in the Netherlands, where they were to work in the control tower at the west end of the rail yard next to a large mining operation. They were to operate the confiscated railroads, transporting troops and supplies from the French ports, and returning with prisoners that had been captured. Only a few miles to the east was Aachen, Germany where the rail yard and tower had been almost completely destroyed by the retreating Germans. It was the first goal of these men to get that yard back into operation and open up the rail line between the two towns. Since railroads were a vital concern to both the Allies and the Germans, the Heerlen tower and yard were still under fire, experiencing frequent strafing by enemy aircraft.

John deviates from his story here to interject a sentiment that he has carried in his heart all these years. He begins by saying that the people of the Netherlands were extremely poor after being under German occupation for so long. Many residents agreed to lodge American GIs in their homes in exchange for food and fuel. John and another telegrapher were quartered in the home of an elderly couple, the man being a retired railroad man. "We called them Mama and Papa de Konig because they were so good to us," he said. "We provided them with coal from the mine and rations from the rail yard. They were so grateful, since they had been living on bread and potatoes and had no fuel much of the time."

After a while, cabooses and baggage cars were converted into living quarters so that the GIs could remain in the rail yard near their work. The railroads and equipment were extremely poor in comparison to the American railroads at that time. Everything was 'link and pin,' no automatic couplers on the cars, and ancient but extremely well made engines. Some modern steam engines that had been liberated from the Germans were later used. The freight cars of the Netherlands were about half the size of American cars and were hazardous due to inadequate brakes. When the railroads were allowed to re-inaugurate their passenger service after the war, it was interesting, to say the least, to see their high-wheeled engines and third class coaches with wooden benches.

As soon as the yard was rebuilt at Aachen, the Allies began to reclaim the rail lines north of Aachen, open and operate that line, and move on up into Germany. John had been serving as a telegraph operator, but was sent to Kassel, Germany, as a train dispatcher under promise of a promotion. His first day as train dispatcher was on his 20th birthday. He said Kassel was the most desolate place he had ever seen, not a single building left standing as the result of the severe bombing.

The men had been living in rail cars during all of this time, but when they got into Hanau, Germany, they occupied homes that had been vacated by evacuated families, and lived quite comfortably until the railroad outfit disbanded at the end of the war. Their work was done. They had reclaimed, rebuilt, and operated the railroads, then turned them back over to the civilians to operate after the armistice.

After the railroad outfit was disbanded, John was assigned a detail of 62 men to take to Antwerp, Belgium to join a group of military police who would be guarding trains. He loves to tell that he was the youngest in the detail, and his rating as staff sergeant was the highest rank of them all.

On their way, they had a layover in Paris. Now, by this time he knew them pretty well, and could almost foretell what a bunch of war-weary GIs would do in Paris. He told them that they must meet him at a certain place at a certain time to leave for Antwerp. Then, in his most authoritative 20-year-old voice, he told them that if they got lost, or misplaced, or even knocked off, he was not going to wait around and worry about them. He reminded them that he had all of their papers in his possession, and he – and their records – would be going to Antwerp as scheduled. They could stay in Paris if they wanted to, but he assured them they wouldn't get very far without their records. In remembering this story, a sly grin came over his face and he said, "And you know, I didn't lose a single man!"

John's rating deserved a 'cushier' job, so he was sent on to Liege, Belgium, and put in charge of a supply room. Working under him was a young Japanese fellow who was being groomed to take over the job. An interesting note is that there were several Japanese men in this battalion. They were U.S. citizens who had been imprisoned in California after the bombing of Pearl Harbor but were released when it was determined that they posed no threat to the country. Also in the supply room was a German prisoner. The prisoners were given jobs to do while they were waiting to be released. The military occupied some large two-story barracks in downtown Liege with Allied soldiers housed in some of them, and German prisoners in others.

With the war over in Europe, it would be a matter of time until the men would be sent home. A point system determined in what order they would be chosen, based on the number of dependents at home, their months of service, and any battle citations they might have. Since John was not married, he could claim no points for dependents, so his points were based on his months of service and three battle citations. Although his outfit was not considered a combat troop, they had been under enemy fire on at least three occasions.

Leaving from LeHavre, where he had arrived about a year and a half earlier, he was on his way home. During the 12 days at sea they were fed Spam sandwiches, Spam sandwiches, and more Spam sandwiches. He recalls that they all thought they would surely starve before they reached the United States, but at least they were headed in the right direction! At the Port of New York, a government inspection was held and the troops were asked if there was anything they needed. To a man, their first and loudest complaint was about how hungry they were. The poor guys were told that they were going back to Camp Kilmer and they would get a good hot meal there. When they reached Camp Kilmer about midnight, the mess hall had been closed – permanently! – and it was almost daylight before they finally got even a cup of coffee. Early the next day, the recruiters began courting them to re-enlist. With a hearty laugh, John remembers that there were not many takers, if any.

Troop trains took the men to Camp Lejeune, North Carolina where they stayed a few days and enjoyed lots of good food, including steak.

John D. Jordan was discharged from the United States Army the day before Mothers Day, 1946, a war veteran before his 21st birthday. After a train ride back to Hahira, Georgia, he gave his sweet mother the best Mothers Day gift she could ever have wished for – her son returning from war, safe and sound.

❖ CHAPTER 3

Frederick P. Wiley

The bombing of Pearl Harbor on December 7, 1941, occurred only about seven months before Frederick Porter Wiley turned 18 years old in July of 1942. The United States was at war. As required by law, Fred had to register for the draft, as did all other 18-year-old males. He was a student at Asbury College in Wilmore, Kentucky, so was deferred for a few months until he completed two years of college.

When time came for him to leave the peaceful little town of Social Circle, Georgia, with its beautiful old high-columned homes and enormous oak trees, he reported to the induction center at Fort McPherson near Atlanta. He recalls experiences of serving on K.P. and guard duty for the few weeks he was there – no soldier's favorite pastime.

Fred was transferred to Camp Wheeler at Macon for 17 weeks of basic training, and after about a month at Fort Meade, Maryland, he was sent to Camp Shanks for embarkation. He docked in Scotland in January 1944, then traveled by train to England. Fred's genteel Southern accent made it sound like a romantic journey as he told me about spending a few nights in a castle at Cornwall, then in a hotel at Marazion, a small town on the coast across from St. Michaels Mount. After a few nights in Penzance at the very southernmost tip of the United Kingdom, he would be sent to the European mainland. While in the U.K. he was assigned to the 29th Division, 175th Infantry, G Company.

By now it was June, 1944. Little did this soft-spoken 19-year-old soldier know, nor could he possibly imagine, what he would soon be facing.

I interrupted Fred at this point when he told me that his

outfit landed in France in June. The first thing that popped into my mind, and out of my mouth was, "Were you at Normandy?" As if to avoid the painful answer, he simply replied, "Yes. We landed at D-plus-one." This meant the day after D-Day, the infamous Normandy invasion. This is where literally thousands upon thousands of our troops were slaughtered by the Germans as American ships emptied their cargo of young men onto the beaches of Northern France.

Trying not to interrupt more than necessary, we sat awhile in silence before he continued: "As we waded ashore, we would trip over what seemed like logs. They were bodies. Among my most vivid memories of that day was......." Again, we sat in silence a few moments while his voice trailed off and he tried to fight back the tears. When he regained his composure, he finished the sentence saying, ".......there was a man's hand lying on the sand." Then he briefly described another horrifying scene where a man had actually been blown through the bottom of a LCVP (a transport) and only half of the body was hanging there.

Later he told me that he didn't know why, after more than half a century, the memory of the hand would still affect him so deeply. This is just another example among the millions of ways that such abhorrent deeds of war can change lives forever.

Artillery fire could be heard in the distance as this wave of troops landed, but there was very little action on the beaches since the Germans had retreated by now. After advancing until almost dark, they found a place to spend the night, then marched the next day on into France. This column of infantrymen was strafed by aircraft fire, and he added that it was believed they were our own planes. Such mistakes as this probably happened more times than we will ever know. With a hint of humor in his voice, he said, "When you are lying in a ditch, those planes look like they are looking right at *you*."

From Normandy, they marched to Saint Lo and were in combat for several weeks trying to break through enemy lines. Fred was slightly wounded, but not severely enough to be pulled from action. About 150 men who were attempting to cross a nearby river were met with gunfire from the Germans. Some were captured, many were killed, and only about 30 got back to camp safely.

After more than a month of fighting, G Company was sent back to a rest area for a break. During this time, the Allies broke through the lines at Saint Lo.

These tired and weary GIs probably thought things couldn't be any worse than what they had already been through. However, when this company went on to Percy, France, Fred's story continues.

They had advanced all day with no opposition, and when they pulled into bivouac at nightfall there was still no sign of Germans anywhere.

Early in the night, Fred decided that the little hole he had dug was not a very good place to sleep and, since there was nothing going on, he and some others went into a nearby barn to sleep. When morning came, the Germans launched a surprise counter-attack and things began to liven up.

The enemy was closing in on them, so one of the soldiers in the barn decided to surrender. The moment he stepped outside, hands in the air, a German bullet shot him down. Fred and the others ran out a rear entrance in an attempt to escape. They had run about 200 yards away from the barn when there was an explosion to their right and a small piece of shrapnel hit Fred in his left eye.

When a doctor looked at him, he was told that he didn't need to be evacuated, but Fred insisted that he had no vision in the eye. After a closer examination, the doctor determined there really was something in the eye, so he put a patch over it and sent him to the aid station, or field hospital.

Fred describes the scene at the hospital where there were lines and lines of wounded. Since he didn't appear to be hurt, *he just couldn't see,* he didn't try to push ahead of the many others who seemed to be in need of help more urgently than himself.

Eventually, a medic who noticed that he had been there for some time with a patch on his eye, called him in to give him some attention. He gave him a place to spend the night, and dismissed him the next morning. It is entirely possible, he told me, that if he had not waited so long for medical help, the outcome might have been different.

There is an old axiom that says you can usually find a little humor in any situation if you just look for it. When Fred began to laugh at this point, especially after such a moving and emotional story as he had just finished telling, it took me aback for a moment. Then he continued.

His outfit was scheduled to go to England that morning. After being dismissed from the aid station, he had waited as long as he could to go to the bathroom, so off he went to find one. While he was gone, his group left for England! He had to catch the next plane he could hail in order to rejoin them.

While there, his eye became so infected that the nurses told him later they had feared for his life, and it was necessary to remove the eye. Penicillin was relatively new at the time but was not used on him, to his knowledge. He was sent to a recuperation area where he received his first artificial eye. Here again he finds humor in the fact that it was a *dentist* who made his first artificial eye, using dental tools and materials.

Back in Social Circle, Fred's mother received a telegram from the War Department informing her that her son had been wounded in action. There were no details other than the fact that he was wounded, but in the first letter she wrote to him after getting the news, she asked him if he had lost an eye. This intriguing story has been told in the family many times through the years. How could she possibly have known! Call it a mother's intuition, call it a message from God, or call it whatever you wish, it is still an amazing story.

While he was recuperating in England, he was able to visit many of the beautiful and historic places in London. When he was fully recovered he was sent back to France. I was shocked and exclaimed, "Sent you back to France!!! They didn't send you home?" In that quiet Southern drawl he said, "Oh no. Even after I had lost an eye, they sent me back to France." I guess they probably needed any warm bodies they could get, since so many of our men had been lost in battle.

He was sent to the 381st M.P. battalion, so at least he did not have to be in actual combat again. He was assigned the job of guarding German prisoners.

At Christmas time 1944, Fred was back in a hospital awaiting orders to go home. In the meantime, however, the bloody Battle of the Bulge had filled all the hospitals to overflowing so he was told he couldn't go home – so he was sent *back* to France! He met two pretty young sisters who were school teachers while he was on town patrol in Nogent-le-Retrou. He and his sister Dorothy corresponded with them for several years before eventually losing contact with them. On at least two occasions, he returned to the little town to visit them. Oh, incidentally, *he didn't bother to get a pass.* After one such rendezvous, he returned to camp only to meet his platoon headed out of town in the opposite direction for relocation. When they saw him coming into town, they stopped. It was on a Sunday, so some of his buddies advised him to tell his officer that he had gone to church. Fred says he doesn't remember just what he did tell the officer, but he doesn't think he used that excuse.

Years later, he met another pretty young school teacher who had moved to Social Circle, but this one didn't get away. He married her. She is my husband's sister.

Fred's story is one of horror and suffering, but he still can laugh at himself. That is a real sense of humor! By this time, I was trying to recall all the times this young renegade of a soldier had been in the wrong place at the wrong time, and was left behind, or almost left behind, and always seemed to get away with it. What makes his stories so funny is that they seem so out-of-character for the Fred Wiley that I know. It's hard to imagine him being so adventuresome.

Earlier, I had listened to some stories of his basic training days in Macon. He said the GIs were allowed to go into town, but nowhere else without a pass. But Fred just couldn't resist hopping a bus for the few miles on up to Social Circle to get a good home cooked meal in his mom's kitchen. One time when he had risked being caught at this trick, the bus failed to run on the return trip. It took a frantic and concerted effort on the part of family and friends to scour up enough gasoline ration stamps, and then to find enough gasoline to drive him back to camp.

After being moved around France to several different locations – by this time, the war had been over in Europe for several months – Fred was again sent to a hospital in Paris and at last was put on a hospital ship to return to the United States. From the port in New Jersey, he was flown to a hospital in Alabama and allowed a furlough for the Thanksgiving and Christmas holidays. What a holiday that must have been for the Wiley family!

When he was discharged from the Army, he resumed his studies at Asbury college, then worked in his family-owned store until he got a job in the post office, working there until he retired in 1980.

By the tender age of 20, he had had several near-death experiences, had witnessed unimaginable horror, and lost an eye from an enemy bomb. What a price to pay for freedom, yet thousands upon thousands paid it, along with those who did not live to tell their story. Those are the names inscribed somewhere among the row upon row upon row of little white crosses.

❖ CHAPTER 4

William H. Camp

Prior to World War II, the U.S. government required all young men to give one year of service to their country. William H. (Bill) Camp had been deferred from this service due to surgery, but immediately after the bombing of Pearl Harbor, he was notified by the draft board that the deferment had been withdrawn.

Bill is the oldest of the veterans mentioned in this book, so he was one of the first in the country to be called into service. Pearl Harbor was attacked on December 7, 1941, and little more than two months later, in February of 1942, Bill found himself at Ft. McPherson, Georgia for induction into the military. Tents had hurriedly been set up to house the recruits, and were soon filled with young men getting ready to leave for parts unknown.

By the month of March in Georgia, the weather is showing signs of Spring, but on the first day of March in 1942, the fort was blanketed with six or seven inches of snow – a rare sight in the South, and not at all what the tent-dwellers needed.

The young men were furnished a little cone shaped heater for their quarters, and some wet green pine to burn in it. The pieces of wood were much too large to fit into the heater, so they chopped it up into smaller pieces and shivered until it dried enough to burn. According to Bill, they shivered afterwards, too.

Many stories have been told of frightened young men trying all kinds of things to prevent being drafted. One of the recruits at Ft. Mac with Bill must have been even more desperate than most. He cut off the forefinger of his right hand, thinking he would be rejected if he couldn't pull the trigger of a gun. The poor guy was processed anyway like all the rest, and was shipped out for basic training with all the others.

Bill was assigned to the Army Air Corps, the predecessor of what later became a separate branch of service known as the Air Force. Jefferson Barracks, Missouri, was his destination for basic training. He relates his thoughts when he was again moved into a tent but this time, at least it had the luxury of a wooden floor. Each tent housed five GIs.

Basic training was intense, which allowed for nothing more than drills, inspections, eating and sleeping. Passes were issued to absolutely no one, so he never left the base.

For the next six months, he was at McDill Field close to Tampa, Florida, attached to the 29th Bomb Group. Following this, he was sent by train, along with the entire 29th, their equipment and personnel, to Gowen Field in Boise, Idaho, and stayed there for several months.

Bill's assignment at Gowen Field was to train flight crews for B-17 bombers being sent to Europe. This included periodically checking and replacing the parachutes that were loaded onto each airplane. He became very efficient at packing the shroud lines, folding the 'chute just right to fit into its canvas cover, and inserting the rip cord and pin carefully and exactly. An airman's life could depend on this precision accuracy.

In August, 1943, he was on his way home for a few days furlough when he received a wire that his father was critically ill. He told me he was thankful that he arrived before his father died, and was even more grateful that he was conscious enough to recognize his son.

Shortly after returning to base, he was placed in the 445th Bomb Group, 701st Squadron. This was a new group being formed in preparation to be sent to Europe. The group was first sent to the Salt Flats in Windover, Utah, where they were joined by another group, and then moved on to Sioux City, Iowa, for another eight weeks of training.

One day he was sent on a preliminary flight to a base in Scribner, Nebraska, before moving equipment and personnel to the base. Casey, the pilot, was coming in for a landing with Bill, who was the flight engineer, between Casey and the co-pilot. He became alarmed when the airplane seemed to be on a crash course right into a corn field with houses nearby. He shouted a warning to the pilot, but ol' Casey was as cool as a cucumber. The scared passenger was told that everything was just fine, and the other two men even seemed to be getting pleasure from the whole thing.

It only took a few moments for Bill to realize that they were approaching a base so well camouflaged that it was almost impossible to spot it from the air. It was built in a large corn field with rows of corn growing right up to the edge of the runways. The buildings and runways were painted in camouflage colors, so skillfully done that it made Bill wonder how his pilot could even find it.

Less than two months after this hair-raising experience, he was shipped overseas. Since their planes had been sent to Europe ahead of them, several thousand troops were loaded onto the luxury liner, the *Queen Mary*. But Bill makes it quite clear that it was no luxury cruise. The ship had been converted to a troop ship but was still serving English cuisine --- kidney stew for breakfast. "Boy, did it smell!" laughs Bill. "Some way to feed us guys that were going over there to keep Hitler from taking their country!"

This Southern boy only made that one trip to the galley and decided he'd rather go hungry. Luckily, he found someone willing to smuggle him some roast beef sandwiches at a dollar apiece until they reached their destination.

In October, 1943, the ship docked in England, just in time for them to be involved in a bombing raid that same night. The men took cover in a huge ditch as fighter planes in dog fights exchanged tracer bullets overhead.

Here the troops were housed in a complex of buildings called Quonset huts, which are metal buildings rounded on top like a half moon. Showers and washing facilities were in the center of the complex, and the mess hall was about half a mile from the sleeping quarters. Also, about a half to three-quarters of a mile away were the runways and taxi stands where the planes were parked.

In England, Bill flight tested planes and was supervisor of the technical supply group. This group supplied the parts for the airplane mechanics.

They had been in England about a year when they were surprised to see a very familiar face assigned to their Group as Squadron Commander for the 703rd Bomb Squadron. He was Capt. Jimmy Stewart. Stewart was a favorite movie star of the era, starring in such classics as *It's A Wonderful Life,* still shown on television in black and white every year at Christmas time, *Mr. Smith Goes to Washington,* and the hilarious *Harvey,* plus dozens more. Bill remembers him as being "very much like you saw him in the movies, slow talking and a real swell fellow."

Each Squadron Commander was required to fly lead plane for his group about once a week. On one of these bombing raids, Stewart's plane returned heavily damaged. With only two working engines, and the fuselage riddled with bullet holes, he landed the plane safely. His co-pilot, gunner, and bombardier were dead. In his quiet manner, he would take no credit for heroism, nor did he want to talk about it at all. Soon afterwards, Stewart was promoted to Major and was transferred to the Wing, a group responsible for planning the bombing raids.

Although Bill was not in a combat outfit, he had some frightening moments and close calls, both while on duty and off. Occasionally he would go by train into London on an off day. It was about a two hour ride from his base near the North Sea. He would usually stay at the Regent Palace Hotel, a nice place that was not very expensive for service men and women.

On one such occasion, it was cold and the snow was falling fast, so he ducked into a pub to get warm. The Germans were firing buzz bombs across the channel and into the city. These were unmanned vehicles that exploded when its fuel supply was exhausted. The fuel was precisely measured to project the bomb an exact distance before falling onto its target. They were also called V-2 rockets.

Bill had walked only a few hundred feet down the street after leaving the pub when a buzz bomb hit the pub he had just left, killing everyone inside. The concussion from the exploding bomb was so strong it knocked him to the sidewalk. Fortunately, he was unhurt. He declares he has never been inside a pub since.

On another occasion, Bill laughs about the only time he was *really* warm while he was in England. He was at his usual hotel, the Regent Palace, and it was a bitterly cold night. He checked into his room and saw that there was only one comforter on his bed. The hotel had no heat, since the war effort demanded all the fuel. He hailed a maid and told her he would freeze to death with so little cover. She assured him he would be comfortable and, after they had 'discussed' the matter thoroughly, he conceded defeat and went to bed, positive that he would spend a miserably cold night. To his surprise, the down comforter felt more like an electric oven, and he thought he would melt before morning came.

In 1945, Bill had completed more than three years in military service. The war in Europe had ended, and the atrocious atomic bombs had been dropped on Japan, so he was sent back to the States on a victory ship to be discharged. Many wounded servicemen were on the ship suffering from all kinds of wounds. Some were unable to walk, others were missing limbs, or still others were sick with fever from infections.

Out in the Atlantic Ocean, the ship ran into a terrific storm and at times it seemed that almost half the ship was submerged in the water. Just about everyone on board was seasick, which added unbearably to the discomfort of the wounded. Those who could make their way to the rails were hanging over the side of the ship. The men had been instructed not to go below to the galley until the storm subsided, which was more than a day. Since the galley is the ship's kitchen, Bill didn't think many of them even had a desire to go in there.

After three years and seven months in the Air Corps, William H. Camp became a civilian again. He insisted his story was not important or interesting enough to include in this book, but I strongly disagreed. Every person had his niche, and it took every one of them working together to save our own country from an invasion by the enemy. Yes, he too is included in my list of heroes.

❖ CHAPTER 5

Virgil Eugene Cheatham, Jr.

Gene Cheatham told me about his war experiences more than fifty years after he had lived through them. After all these years, my maturity and having taught about WW II in my classroom, made me want to know *everything* he could tell me. So, with my tape recorder in hand, I prompted his story from him. It was this story that gave me the desire to tell the other stories you will read in this book.

He was the second oldest son in the family with whom I lived after the death of my parents. I well remember his homecoming, but I never asked any questions. Because I was just a child, I mostly stayed out of the way and observed while my aunt, his mother, hovered over him and tended to his needs. I remember that it was too painful for even the bed sheet to touch his feet and legs. There he lay, his handsome face and farmboy-strong body practically helpless, wasting away, and in agony.

Virgil E. Cheatham, Jr., was born on June 26, 1925, and had to register for the draft in 1943, as every young man did on his 18th birthday. He was ordered to report for duty in March 1944 to Fort McPherson, GA. Due to an accident a few days before reporting, he sustained an injury that required a brief hospital stay at Fort Mac before he was sent to Fort Knox, Kentucky, for 13 weeks of basic training. After a 14-day furlough home, and a three-day stay at Fort Smith, Arkansas, he was sent to Camp Kilmer, New Jersey, and shipped directly overseas. He recalls that after only about 18 weeks in the U.S. Army, he found himself in combat, just barely 19 years old.

A group of men who took basic training together was sent overseas together where they were assigned to the 1st Army under the command of Gen. Courtney Hodges. Here they were divided into groups. When a name was called, that man was to move to the right. When the list of names was completed, one of his buddies from basic was not included. With a compassionate heart and a lot of nerve, Gene stepped up to the officer and asked if, by any chance, Chestnutt's name was overlooked. It was. So Chestnutt was allowed to move to the right to be with his buddies from basic training.

A second roll call separated the men into two regiments. All whose names were called this time went into the 33rd Armored Regiment, 3rd Armored Division. The others were to become the 32nd Regiment. This time it was Gene whose name was not called, so he went into the 32nd not knowing a single man. He added with a grin, "But when you're facing the unknown, you'll find you a good buddy pretty fast."

The 32nd Regiment was in a small village in Germany around December 12 when they were suddenly ordered down to Eupen, Belgium, to reinforce a weak point in the line. For three days they sat in the edge of Eupen being fired upon by German V-2 rockets. These were extremely sensitive and powerful gasoline powered bombs engineered to explode when a precisely measured amount of fuel burned out, hopefully right on target, or when hitting the slightest obstacle. After some time, Gene drew watch to allow the others to get some sleep. On his watch, he spotted one of these bombs headed directly toward his tank. He quickly ordered the men to buckle the hatches and lock the tracks. No sooner had this been done than the bomb barely cleared them, exploding just beyond a small tree they were parked under, knocking that monstrous tank about four feet from where it had been sitting.

Later that same night, December 15, the company commander, who probably thought he needed a stiff drink by this time, decided to break into the half-track load of cognac he had stored up for the guys to have for Christmas. He may have felt, too, that there might not be a Christmas for some of them. Thinking the Germans had done all they were going to do for the night, he allowed the company to have all the booze they wanted.

Except for Gene, who was not a drinking man, the entire company promptly got stinkin' drunk.

At 5:30 on the morning of the 16th, the Germans broke through at Luxembourg, so the Division was ordered to move from Belgium to Luxembourg. These guys, drunk as could be, drove all day. They reached what they thought was their destination in Luxembourg about dark. Gene looked out and all he could see was enemy tanks and Germans. They realized they were 18 miles inside enemy lines! This should have been enough to sober them up, and through some miracle, they were able to get out of there and back into Allied territory.

In preparation for the combat they were to face the following day, fuel was trucked in to them, but the guys were still so drunk and hung over that the truck drivers would not bring the fuel out to the tank. Knowing that they could not go into combat without refueling, Gene took two five-gallon cans, one in each hand, and made 14 trips across a field, manually loading 140 gallons of fuel into the tank.

It had rained all night and the rain was turning to snow. By 9 o'clock in the morning, the snow was already knee deep. Gene was soaking wet after manually and singlehandedly refueling the tank, and he told the others he couldn't possibly go into combat like that. He must dry his clothes. So the whole company drove into a small nearby town, gathered some rubble, built a big fire, and stripped Gene down to his skin. There in the middle of town they dried his clothes while he stood stark naked by the fire. He explains that modesty doesn't play a large role in times like these.

As scheduled, they were sent out that day and met heavy enemy fire, the beginnings of some of the most atrocious battles of the war in Europe. Our history books call this period *The Battle of the Bulge.*

On Christmas Eve, Gene recalls that the sky overhead was so black with hundreds upon hundreds of airplanes that they all felt sure the war could not last many more days. Christmas Day was spent in Marche, Belgium.

The fighting continued to rage and within the week following Christmas Day, his company was almost completely wiped out. As was the practice, these survivors had to be assigned to another company. They regrouped, and there in northern Belgium around the first day of January, Gene Cheatham began the greatest nightmare of his life.

Here, they were met with such heavy fire that they were unable to escape the confines of that armored tank. For seven days and seven nights they were trapped inside with no relief from the barrage of artillery. The weather was bitterly cold.

During this time, several small towns were captured, and they were then called to Lierneux, south of Liege, Belgium. The history books tell us that Richardson's task force was caught in heavy fighting trying to take Lierneux and needed help. So, Hogan's taskforce, of which Gene was a part, was sent as backup for Richardson's men.

Down a field road and across a concrete bridge, Hogan's boys and their tanks then entered a large pasture. Seeing the heavy barrage of bullets flying across the open field, Gene compared the sight to a huge swarm of bees. Later, you will read these exact words from others who also compared the heavy artillery fire to swarms of bees.

When Hogan's reinforcements arrived and began firing, German soldiers by the hundreds emerged from the woods to their left, waving white cloths over their heads. Gene rather emotionally related the following story:

> "When I saw all those guys surrendering, I don't know why I did it, but I prayed that now they would be safe and no more of them would be hurt. When I did, I felt a firm but gentle grip on my right shoulder. I thought, 'Whoa, there's nothing behind me but 2 inches of solid steel!' Right then I realized that if God could reach me behind those solid plates of steel, He could be with me anywhere."

Gene's tank was named 'Irene' because his company was "I" Company. All day long, 'Irene' was the front tank in battle. They advanced over a hill late in the day and began to pick up a radio message. The voice was saying in English, but with a German accent, "Turn right, Irene. Turn right, Irene." Hoping the Allies would think the command was from one of their own, the Germans were attempting to get the Allied tanks in position to be fired upon. Not falling for the scheme, the tanks continued over another hill and found themselves in another open field just as before. Artillery fire was heavy, and again the sky was literally black with bullets. Although the Allies were victorious and captured the field, 17 tanks had entered this battle, but only two returned – the tank Gene was in, and one other.

On their way back to town, they could see thousands of German soldiers swarming across a mountainside, but they were not so concerned about them because they were foot soldiers who were dug in for their own protection.

It was dark and extremely cold on that night, January 5, 1945, when the two remaining tanks pulled into a grove of trees at the edge of a town. From this time until late the next afternoon, Gene has no memory of anything that happened. It could have been fatigue, or it could have been shock, but he remembers nothing for almost 24 hours.

The next thing he remembers, they pulled the tanks out of the woods onto a railroad track, traveled down the tracks, and came to a railroad station. Some of the men went inside to scout out the building and came back to report that there were some beds in the basement. It was decided to flip a coin to see who would stand guard at the tank the first two hours of the night while the others went in to get some sleep. Gene lost the coin toss and was assigned guard duty.

He got out of his assistant driver's seat and climbed up into the turret to man the guns. *This was the first time he had been on his feet in seven days and nights!* Thinking the pain in his feet was from lack of circulation, he spent the two hours of his watch on his knees.

An interview with anyone else probably would not have prompted my next question, but being close family, inquisitive, wanting to know *everything,* hoping to convey the complete story, I asked it anyway. He said he was in that tank for seven days and nights, no coffee breaks and no restroom facilities. How did he, well, you know, uh, how did he manage that? I really would like to quote him verbatim on this matter because his answer was frank and detailed, to say the least. However, to keep the story acceptable to all readers, I'll paraphrase his words!

In a nutshell, when a person is so horribly frightened, bodily functions either cease or increase. His completely ceased, but some of the other men in the tank were not so fortunate. He goes on to describe the situation, and says he still can remember just how good it felt "when things got back to normal." He definitely had a way with words. But I had asked for it, hadn't I!

When he was relieved of his duty he was told where to go to find the beds, but finding them occupied, he climbed up onto a pile of hay and pulled off his shoes. His feet were really painful by this time so, still believing that the pain was from lack of circulation, he tried to put his shoes back on so he could walk around. He couldn't get them on. His next thought was to walk around in his bare feet. When he tried to get up, first on his right foot and then on his left, it was impossible for him to get up into a standing position.

In the total darkness, Gene pulled a blanket over himself and shined a flashlight on his feet so he could see what was wrong. They were swollen many times their normal size. He remembers thinking how thankful he was that his parents couldn't see him, sitting here in the midst of enemy territory in such a condition. His feet and legs were severely frozen.

"I" Company had to pull out early the next morning and leave Gene behind. Living in the basement of this railroad station, trying to escape the Germans, were a man, his wife, two boys, and a grandmother. This family did not hesitate to offer to care for him. They had nothing but potatoes to eat, but they generously shared with him what they had.

Caring for him throughout the night, one of the women constantly bathed the frozen feet and legs in warm water, a technique that was much opposed in U.S. medical practice for treating severe frostbite at that time.

When it was daylight, the woman sent her husband out to

find some morphine. He encountered a lieutenant and told him he needed some morphine for a soldier. Suspecting that they were harboring a German soldier, the lieutenant took two GIs with him to investigate. With a GI on either side of his bed, M-1 rifles cocked and pointed at his temples, Gene was questioned extensively. As he had been trained to do, he did not answer. The officer then asked such questions as what ball team played where or when, and what was the score. Finally Gene was so agitated and in such pain, he blurted out, "Hell, man, how would I know – I'm from *Paulding County, Georgia!"* The officer immediately realized that no German in the world could possibly mimic that Southern drawl with a mountaineer's accent, and that is probably what saved his life!

The woman in the railway station wanted Gene to be left in her care, but of course the officer could not do that. He picked up the crippled soldier and carried him on his back to get medical attention. Some of the family went along to help. With the woman holding the suffering boy's hand, they all risked their own lives amid bursting artillery fire for at least 30 minutes until the field ambulance arrived. She did not leave his side until he was safely loaded and taken away. He repeated emotionally, "She held my hand the whole time."

He was taken to a hospital in Paris where he witnessed, in his words, "the most pitiful sight" he has ever seen in his entire life. There he heard wounded men crying and calling "Mama! Mama!" Having a son of my own, I could hardly bear even the thought of such a scene, and I interjected, "Bless their hearts, and most of them were probably just teenagers." In a calm, quiet voice he remarked, "Yeah, just about my age."

That jerked me back to the reality that all of this had not happened to that white haired old man that was sitting across the table from me. It happened to "just a teenager."

Gene reverts at this point to ask if I had ever read the essay, *Footprints.* I had.

A man dreamed he was walking along a beach with God, leaving two sets of footprints in the sand. At the end of his dream he looked back over his life and noticed that in the

lowest and worst times, there was only one set of footprints. He questioned God as to why He would leave him alone when He was needed most. The Lord answered his question by telling him, "When you see only one set of footprints, it was then that I was carrying you." (*Author unknown*)

Gene asks if I remembered him telling me about the 20 or so hours that was a total blank to him. I did. He said he believes that was when God was carrying him, laying him aside until He had just the right person and place for the care he needed. That was the women in the basement of the railroad station. He learned many years later that one of them had been a nurse during World War I and had cared for Charles de Gaulle when he was a lieutenant in the French army.

By the time Gene left Europe, it was April. He was loaded onto a hospital ship in England for the long sea voyage home. The ship docked in New York on April 13th, the day after the death of President Roosevelt on the 12th. For a country to be shocked by such news as the death of its president is devastating enough --- but a country *at war!* What would we do? Even among the wounded on that hospital ship, this was a topic of grave concern.

When they docked in New York, there were ambulances lined up "for miles" to take the hundreds of wounded to hospitals. Each ambulance could accommodate two patients. The other patient in the ambulance with Gene had a temperature of 107 degrees. Since this constituted an emergency, that ambulance was given clearance and was one of the first to arrive at a hospital.

A well-dressed man and an American officer were standing nearby as the two soldiers were being unloaded. The man began asking Gene questions, but again, as he had been trained to do, he would not answer. The officer leaned over him and gently assured him that everything was okay, he was back in the States now, and he could answer the man's questions. He was a newspaper reporter gathering information on the reactions and comments regarding the death of FDR. He asked the soldier's name and where he was when he heard the news.

As was the practice of the *New York Times* during the war, their headlines were almost half a page tall. The following morning the headlines read, **"WOUNDED AT FRONT, HEARS NEWS AT SEA."**

The story was picked up by newspapers all over the world, and reached Paulding County, Georgia, via *The Atlanta Journal.* That is how Gene's parents found out that this son was safely back in the States.

He was allowed to call home when he arrived at a hospital at Camp Butner in North Carolina. His father told my aunt that they could be ready to leave the next day to go to see him. She answered, "If you are going with me, you'd better get ready to leave NOW!" And they did.

Doctors continued to say that Gene's feet must be amputated, but all the while they seemed to be improving. After seven months and ten days in the hospital, he was released. Although he continued to suffer much pain, he still had his own two feet. It would take many years to recover to the degree that he enjoys today, even though it is less than 100 percent.

In 1950, during the Korean War, a letter arrived from the Veterans Administration requesting Gene to report to Emory Hospital in Decatur, Georgia, near Atlanta, for tests and questioning. His records showed how severely his feet and legs were damaged, and yet it had not been necessary to amputate them, so the doctors wanted to find out just what was done for him when he first received help. They were in hopes of saving men who were experiencing the same injury in Korea.

The doctors were astounded when they learned that the very method of treatment they had always forbidden in treating this injury was exactly what the Belgian woman had used, which was bathing his feet and legs constantly for hours in warm water. Because of the results of her simple method, the medical books were completely rewritten regarding the treatment of what they call severe frostbite.

All through these years, Gene had often remarked that it was his deep desire to go back to Europe and find that caring family. Of course he wanted to thank them, but he also wanted to let them know that they not only saved him, but possibly countless others as well. He wanted to somehow give them the credit they deserved.

In a later chapter you will learn more about this yearning, and how Gene sought to fulfill this desire that he had carried in his heart for more than 50 years.

PART THREE

Pacific Theater of Operations

❖ CHAPTER 6

William A. Cheatham

Thus far in this book, we have looked at the experiences of those who served in the European Theater of Operations. Now we will go halfway around the world and take a look at what was going on in the Pacific Theater. That conflict lasted longer than the war in Europe, and it was there that the first blood was shed with the bombing of Pearl Harbor in Hawaii on December 7, 1941.

William A. (Bill) Cheatham is the oldest son of my aunt with whom I lived. He and his siblings grew up as brothers and sisters to my siblings and me. He is the brother of Gene Cheatham whose story you read in a previous chapter.

Bill was notified to report for induction in April, 1943 after registering for the draft in April, 1942. He reported to the draft office expecting to be sent directly to the induction center, but when roll was called, his name was not included. He went into an office and informed them that his name had not been called. After a thorough check, it was affirmed that he was not on the list. Bill reached into his pocket and took out his greetings, as the notification papers were 'affectionately' called, to show that he had been notified to report on that date. Somewhat puzzled, the clerk began to investigate. It was discovered that Bill had applied for a deferment earlier because his dad needed him on the farm, and a mixup had occurred in his paper work. He must have looked astounded, so the clerk told him that if he really wanted to go that day, they could certainly arrange it! So he signed an affidavit to withdraw the appeal for deferment, and found himself at Fort McPherson within two hours listening to somebody tell him what to do.

Momentarily, this young farm boy wondered if he had done the right thing, but he quickly added that he really knew it was exactly what he should have done.

From Fort Mac, he was sent to a new base that had just recently opened in Greensboro, North Carolina, called Basic Training Camp (BTC) #10. Mainly, for about five weeks, he went through close order drill and basic training. He was then interviewed and assigned to a school for heavy equipment operators in Fort Belvoir, Virginia, then to Salt Lake City, Utah, and on to Geiger Field in Spokane, Washington. He was Army personnel, but was attached to the Air Corps, a predecessor of the United States Air Force.

At Geiger Field, he was assigned to the 866th Aviation Engineer Battalion. In reminiscing, he told me that this battalion has an Engineers Club which meets every two years in Davenport, Iowa. Of course, many of the men are no longer with them, but those who are left still enjoy getting together.

Bill arrived at Geiger Field later than the rest of his outfit, so he was shipped to another air base in the state of Washington until they regrouped. They were then sent to a bivouac area on the Columbia River where an airstrip was being built. This was a part of the training, since the purpose of this outfit was to build and maintain airstrips.

After a short trip back to Geiger Field, they went on to Desert Center, California, where the temperature was 118 degrees in the shade when they got off the train.

He was moved from one base to another until he finally left the United States for New Guinea on his 21st birthday, April 22, 1944. He won his freedom as an adult, he says, watching San Francisco slip out of sight.

New Guinea is a large island north of Australia in the Pacific Ocean. He spent more time on this island than any one place while he was in the Pacific. Since they were continuously moving, it was more or less their point of operations.

The island of Leyte in the central part of the Philippine Islands was the focal point of the U.S. invasion of the Philippines in 1944. It was the first island recaptured after the Japanese had taken it earlier. The 866th AEB was sent to Leyte and encountered their first combat at sea en route. Leyte had been secured by that time, so the Engineers had some serious repairs to make on the island.

In December, 1944, after they had completed that project, they were loaded onto LSTs and were informed that they would be going to the island of Mindoro, about 450 miles to the northwest. They did not know it at that time, but this was referred to as a suicide mission. It has since been declared one of the boldest invasions of the war in the Pacific.

Winding through the small Japanese infested Philippine Islands, the trip took about four days. They were always in sight of land with Japanese suicide planes sitting on ready. They were under enemy bombing attacks all the while. One of the escort ships in their convoy, the *USS Nashville*, was heavily damaged by Kamikaze planes and suffered several hundred casualties.

Manila, the capital of the Philippines, was one of the Japanese strongholds, so it would be to the Allies' advantage to base their airplanes closer to it. Since Mindoro is only 150 miles south of Manila, this was the place chosen for an airbase, but first they must claim the island. Also, Mindoro is a main island in the Philippines, only 500 miles from the coast of China. By taking it, major sea and air routes could be opened to China.

This was deep within Japanese territory, so the invasion of Mindoro was expected to be a bloody excursion, much the same as the invasion of Normandy Beach in Europe had been earlier in the year. The troops were instructed to take five days of food with them, and nothing else, in preparation for the long battle. The site chosen for the airfield was about five miles inland. Expecting to cover a mile a day was being optimistic.

The invasion of Mindoro took place at dawn on December 15, 1944, and although the Engineers found themselves under fire, mainly from the air, the fighting was not as severe as had been expected as they made their taskforce landing. They were heavily supported by the Navy's ships and PT boats, which diverted attention from the land troops. It was a fierce battle, but the fighting was mostly sea-to-air combat.

Another element in favor of the Allied troops was that the Japanese had been taken by surprise.

The job of the Engineers was to build an airstrip on the island and they were ordered to have it completed in 15 days. Working night and day, surrounded by infantrymen and paratroopers for protection, the airstrip was ready to accommodate aircraft in only eight days.

All this activity was taking place only 75 miles off the coast of Japanese-held Luzon, seven weeks before it was invaded by the Allies on January 9, 1945. It is difficult to imagine how U.S. troops were able to build an airstrip *400 miles inside enemy territory,* and only 150 miles from Manila.

From this airstrip on Mindoro, paratroops and supplies were airlifted to Corregidor on C-46 and C-47 transport bombers, which were slow-moving cargo planes. Corregidor and the Bataan Peninsular in Manila Bay had been captured by the Japanese in 1942, and the Allies desperately needed to regain possession of those strategic positions.

Paratroops from Mindoro landed on the island of Corregidor on February 16, 1945, and with ships and planes joining in the heavy fighting, the Allies were successful in recapturing it, but not before many lives were lost in the effort.

It was later learned that there were an estimated 20 Japanese airstrips in the area that could have swallowed up the Engineers during the time they were working on Mindoro. It seems pretty clear that it was not *humanly* possible for our troops to survive in this position. "It was the Lord's protection," Bill says humbly. It seems that the Almighty just made our boys invisible to the enemy.

Bill believes that this one project, if no other, was his purpose for being there. His outfit definitely contributed immeasurably as a turning point in the Pacific war. His unit was awarded the medal for meritorious service and was nominated for a presidential award, which never came through.

The Engineers Club a few years ago, acquired some information into those operations, which at the time of the action were extremely top secret. For about 18 months no one knew where they were located except that they were "somewhere in the Pacific."

From Mindoro, he was sent to Manila after its occupation by the Allies and, as heavy equipment operator, helped prepare the groundwork for an enormous general hospital. The proposed facility was to cover about 800 acres and was in preparation for the invasion of Japan. When this job was about half completed, the atomic bombs were dropped on Japan, and work on the hospital, as well as the war, came to a halt. The invasion of Japan, thankfully, was not necessary.

Bill said he had mixed feelings for a lot of years about the use of the atomic bomb, but after studying many sources, he knows there was no other way to bring the war to an end. Now he is at peace with himself about it.

When Bill came home, he had what was known as 'jungle rot' on both feet. Sometimes they looked as if his toes would fall off. It was caused from the continuous moisture and heat. Their shoes were a type of canvas which would supposedly allow more air circulation than leather; however, they made it impossible to keep his feet dry. When he got home they completely healed and he has had no more problems.

These young men occasionally could find a little humor to relieve the hell they suffered. He laughs about a time when several of the guys desperately needed a good hot shower. They took a spreader, which is a piece of equipment that sprays asphalt through small holes along extended arms several feet long, and filled the huge kettle with water from the river. They lit the burners, heated the water, and lined up under those sprayers for what they expected to be a much-longed-for shower. Much to their surprise, the spreader was not *new* equipment, as they had thought, and they found themselves coated with asphalt. To make matters worse, they had to clean themselves with gasoline, which doesn't do a lot for your skin!

"Can you remember where you were when you heard the news of the president's death?" I asked. He was on the job operating a large piece of equipment.

He remembers that the way he found out Gene was back in the States was a newspaper article someone sent him. It was the article quoting Gene at the hospital in New York when he had been asked to comment on the death of FDR. He is not sure how old the article was by the time he received it, because communications from the States were slow. He knew of two men in his outfit whose wives had died 30 days before the news caught up with them.

I asked Bill if he had ever compared dates with his brother, Gene, to see what was going on with the two of them at any given time. He had not so I made some comparisons myself:

During the week of December 12 through 17, 1944, Bill was at sea en route to the island of Mindoro, under Japanese attack on the way. At dawn on the 16th he was involved in the bold invasion of the island. Gene had experienced an attack from German V-2 rockets at Eupen, Belgium, on the 15th. On the 17th he was caught in some of the first bloody fighting in the Battle of the Bulge.

The brothers were both in harm's way at exactly the same time, a world apart.

Bill ends our interview by saying, "I had to become a Christian to learn Who won the war, and I had to become a father to find out who paid the greatest sacrifice."

❖ CHAPTER 7

Joseph O. Simmons

You have read the stories of veterans who served in various capacities: the infantry, a railroad battalion, in an armored tank, an aviation engineer, and the Army Air Corps. Now let's turn to the United States Marine Corps.

Joseph O. (Joe) Simmons jokes that he had been brainwashed by John Wayne and Dorothy Lamour, famous movie stars at the time, whose films glorified the U.S. Marines. That was what Joe wanted to do, so when he finished high school, he was ready to go. Since he was only 17 years old, his parents would not agree to sign the written permission required for under age volunteers. Just as soon as he was 18, he joined the Marines rather than being drafted into another branch of service. This was the summer of 1943.

He was processed at Fort McPherson in Atlanta, as were most of the young men from Georgia, was put on a Greyhound bus, and sent to Paris Island, South Carolina, for 12 weeks of boot camp. During the next 12 weeks, he learned to fire just about every kind of weapon available at that time. Then, he was sent to Camp Lejeune, North Carolina, for several weeks of training in communications.

I interrupted him and asked just what that involved, and he began by telling me he learned to use a radio. I must have looked puzzled. My thoughts were racing, wondering how much training it took for these macho guys to learn to turn a knob or push a button!

He went on to say it would be hard to imagine just what they were like compared to what we have now. This was before the days of transistors, and the battery-operated piece of equipment that was used was so heavy it took two men to carry it, and it stayed out of order about half the time, he said.

Also, they had to learn semafore, a system of arm positions, each representing a certain letter of the alphabet. Sometimes colored flags were held in each hand for better visibility. He admitted he never got very good at sending semafore signals, but he did learn the letters of the alphabet and could read an incoming message.

Joe went on to explain that he watched guys signaling between ships at sea when other means of communication were not safe, and he could see that it was a valuable skill to have. He said he was never in a situation where it was necessary, but it was good to know that in case someone tried to intercept a communication, messages could be relayed in silence.

I asked him to go back to boot camp and tell me a little about that. I've always heard the Marines were so-o-o tough, and I wanted to hear what he could tell me about it. His first comment was that it quickly separated the men from the boys. He had seen guys enter training weighing 230 pounds and leave only a few weeks later weighing 180.

Their regular daily routine began at 5 a.m. by running an obstacle course before breakfast, followed by about 12 hours of intense physical exercise, and getting to bed around 10 o'clock at night. He laughs that the guys who were overweight lost weight, and the guys who were underweight gained weight through muscle building, so they all looked alike when they left there. To prove his point, he told me that they were not even issued uniforms until training was over, because of size changes. He didn't change much, he said, because he was pretty slender and in good shape when he went in. However, he did gain some weight because he ate everything he could get his hands on, including plain bread, after such a workout.

Joe was then sent to Camp Pendleton, California, where intensive training was given in tactics that might be needed in actual combat. They practiced abandoning ship by jumping into water from a height of 35 feet wearing all of their equipment. They learned how to use a bayonet in hand-to-hand combat, and other survival techniques they might need.

After being sent to Hawaii for about 10 days, he went to Guadalcanal in the Solomon Islands. It was here that the first offensive action of WW II had been fought and won by the United States in 1942-43.

Even after the occupation, which had already taken place before this wave of Marines arrived, there were many Japanese still holed up in the hills. The troops patrolled during the day looking for them, at the same time learning how to maneuver in jungle combat. Their campsite was patrolled at night to prevent a possible attack. He explained how a Japanese soldier could sneak into the GIs' tents and, using a piece of piano wire, wrap it around a man's neck and kill him silently. Not awakening anyone around him, he would go to the next, and to the next.

Their tour of duty then took them to Guam, where he was assigned to the 6th Marine Division and sent to Okinawa in the northern Pacific, very close to the Japanese mainland. Three divisions of Marines were to take the southern end of the island of Okinawa, and the Army was assigned the northern part. Three other divisions of Marines were sent to Iwo Jima, where some of the heaviest fighting and bloodshed of the Pacific war took place.

As we have learned from history books, there was a tremendous loss of lives on Iwo Jima. About half the men Joe knew from boot camp were among those killed. This is just one of the untold numbers of personal experiences our *im*personal history books cannot possibly convey.

The night before the invasion of Okinawa was Easter Sunday, 1945, and a chaplain conducted a small service on the ship. "Everybody had religion that night," he remembers, but then he got very somber as he continued. The speaker told the men to take a long look at their buddy because "one of you won't be coming back." It was predicted that at least half of those men would lose their lives. Joe remarked that, even though those words seemed a bit absurd to him at the time, the speaker was being realistic. It was a graphic reminder that they could not take any chances. They were told not to try to be a hero, but use their heads and do their best to be around when it was all over. Joe added, "Obviously, there were a lot of us who were not."

Before they were to land on Okinawa, the U.S. Navy bombed the beaches in order to detonate any land mines that might be buried in the sand. He said it was interesting, to say the least, to watch from the anchored ships off shore as the Japanese Kamikaze pilots were bearing down on them through the heavy Navy artillery fire. Although it seemed impossible for a plane to get through it, some of them did. He said he once knew how many ships the Allies lost in that attack, but he has forgotten. There were quite a few, however.

He was not sent to Iwo Jima, but Okinawa was, as he phrased it, "a messy situation" also. The civilians were held hostage by Japanese soldiers and they all ran to the end of the island, refusing to surrender. The Marines had no choice but to annihilate them all. Unfortunately, the civilians could not be distinguished from the soldiers because they all wore the same type of kimono-like garments. Many people were slaughtered unnecessarily but, because there possibly could be concealed weapons underneath those loose garments, no chances could be taken. "As horrible as it may sound, sadly, that's what war is all about," he said.

The Marines threw phosphorous grenades onto the roofs of houses and burned them down. Buildings that seemed empty, many times had Japanese snipers hiding inside and, again, they could take no chances.

After 82 blood-soaked days of fighting, the island of Okinawa finally fell to the Allies. The fighting continued, however, for about two more weeks as the last of the Japanese were flushed out of hiding. More than 10,000 men were killed and 25,000 wounded.

After 100 hellish days on Okinawa, these troops returned to Guam to prepare for the invasion of the Japanese mainland. The atomic bomb was actually dropped on Hiroshima, Japan, while Joe was on Okinawa, but the Japanese did not surrender right away. They continued to attack with their suicide planes. The second atomic bomb was dropped before they surrendered, and the peace treaty was signed on September 2, 1945.

Sometime in April during the Okinawa campaign, a well known and well liked news correspondent by the name of Ernie Pyle was killed by a Japanese sniper. He had been covering the European war, and this was his first assignment in the Pacific.

These tired, battle-weary troops then were shipped to Tokyo Bay where they sat for three days under Japanese fire. They were waiting for Gen. Douglas McArthur to arrive to negotiate the peace treaty. It was typhoon season, and rough seas prevented his seaplane from coming in as scheduled.

When the treaty was signed, the U.S. ships were moved into a large Japanese naval base where the Marines made a startling discovery. They found hundreds of small row boat size motor boats with a torpedo attached to each bow, intended to ram any U.S. ships that came into the harbor. One history book called them "Q boats," although I do not know why. The pilot of the small boat had a mission, and that was to kill, knowing that he would die as well. This was similar to the Kamikaze pilot, wired into his bomb-laden airplane, his body attached to weights to take him to the bottom of the sea when his plane dived into a ship. He was considered sacred if he died for the Emperor. It was the belief of the Japanese that these acts of heroism would earn them a place in heaven.

Joe went on to tell me that, by the time these little suicide boats were discovered, the Japanese had cut every one of them in two. It was a sight to see, at least two or three hundred of them, and also a terrible feeling to know that "one of them might have had my name on it."

They were soon sent back to Guam, then sailed back into Tokyo Bay, and disembarked at Yokosuka Naval Base. The buildings were clean and modern, and inside they found dozens of comfortable-looking hammocks. Every man immediately picked out a hammock for himself, envisioning a long overdue and much-needed rest.

Suddenly, someone had the thought that this could be a trap. The Japanese wouldn't hesitate to come in and wipe them out while they slept, even though the treaty had been signed. So, instead of sleeping, they went outside and dug foxholes, three men to each, and spent the night in shifts, with one man on watch while two slept.

Morning came and nothing had happened, so they went further onto the naval base. They found dead Japanese lying everywhere, most likely a mass suicide since the Japanese believed it was a disgrace to be captured or to surrender. The Marines were ordered to disarm the bodies and take them to a central deposit area where, it was Joe's guess, they were probably burned. Each Marine was given a Japanese pistol and a rifle to send home as souvenirs, if they wished. Most of them did. Joe kept his for years but disposed of it because ammunition was not available except to order it from Japan.

The troops were sent to Tokyo where they were required to march through the devastated city as a show of force. It is no surprise that they were met with expressions of anger, hatred, and sadness on the face of everyone they saw.

After the war, enough powder and ammunitions were found stored in caves in the area to equip the Japanese for many more years of fighting. Had it not been for the atomic bomb, Joe says with assurance that he and hundreds of thousands of others, including Japanese, would not have survived much longer. It was a necessary evil.

After being there 21 days, Gen. McArthur arrived. Joe told me that, to a man, Marines hated McArthur's guts. (Then he paused, grinned, and added, "Well, maybe you'll find a chaplain that doesn't feel that way.")

He went on to say that a young Marine of Mexican origin had been assigned guard duty at the entrance to one of the caves, and his orders were to let no one – *no one* – inside the cave. Along comes this 5-star general with his entourage of 10 or 12 lieutenants, adjutants, etc., expecting to go in to inspect the cave. The young guard says, "You don't go in there. Nobody goes in the cave."

One of the dignitaries stepped up to the young man, and in a rather sarcastic tone said that he surely must know who this man is. He is *Gen-e-ral-Doug-las-Mc-Ar-thur,* and he wants to go into the cave. Assuming port arms position, that brave little

Marine answered, "I don't give a damn *who* he is. Nobody goes into the cave unless my orders are changed!" They obediently halted and waited for new orders to arrive.

A spark from McArthur's corncob pipe could have made the atomic bomb unnecessary.

The next day they received orders to go back to Guam for the third time – McArthur just didn't know what on earth to do with a bunch of guys like this. It was decided to send them to China to transport Japanese soldiers back to the mainland. Some of them had been fighting the Chinese Nationalists for years.

One of the most unjust things that Joe feels happened to him during his service was on a ship headed for home. "Unjust" (his definition) because nothing was ever done to the perpetrators. The incident had nothing to do with the war, but after what these guys had been through, it does seem that the outcome was unjust.

The Marines had their service pistols well protected in their sea bags in preparation for the voyage home. At sea, the sailors (Joe had another name for them!) cut out the bottom of the sea bags and took their pistols. Not only did they lose a valuable possession, but their bags were ruined and had to be taped together. Also, their belongings had fallen out and were damaged. Their sea bags were ruined, their belongings were damaged, and their pistols were gone. The furious men went to the ship's captain with the matter and were told that there was nothing he could do about it. Nothing he could do about it??? They were contained on board a ship on the high seas, and there was nothing he could do about it!!! Joe believes the captain might have received a share of the valuable weapons, himself.

I have asked each of the men I interviewed if they could tell me of their most narrow escape with death, or their most frightening experience. Joe didn't hesitate to let me know that was an easy question. He had several close calls – everybody did – but one in particular really scared him

He and a buddy were in some woods on the island of Okinawa and were attempting to cross a clearing into another wooded area. Suddenly a "Screaming Willie" was fired right at them. A Screaming Willie, as the GIs called them, was a 15-inch

Japanese artillery shell that emitted a loud, shrill scream as it sailed through the air. The shell hit the ground about 10 yards from the two men, then bounced up, going over their heads, and landing a short distance away. Fortunately, the shell was a dud. The men would have been blown to bits, had it been live.

The Japanese had lots of faulty ammunition, but they also had lots of tricks up their sleeves. One of their favorites was to position a sniper up in a tree. He would quietly wait for a group of troops to pass by, and when the last man in the group passed, who was the commanding officer, the sniper would shoot him. Of course, the troops turned around and filled the sniper full of holes, but that was just what he wanted – now he would go to heaven like the Kamikaze and boat heroes.

The men could never let their guard down. They never knew when a sniper would come out of a cave or out of a house and start firing. But war is war, as these men will tell you, and death is staring them in the face at every turn. That is just to be expected in combat.

I asked how his family found out he was on his way home. He wasn't sure about that, but they had no idea where he was for months before, except that he was "somewhere in the Pacific." They did know that he was with the 6th Marine Division, so later when *Time* magazine, or *Newsweek,* or other news sources picked up a story about the 6th Division, they at least knew where those troops were. Of course, they would still have no news about their son, personally.

Probably, any serviceman could tell of various experiences covering everything from near-death to humor, and Joe is certainly no exception. He told of leaving his carbine (weapon) on the ground and it was run over in the dark by a Jeep, breaking the gunstock. He was docked $27 from his check to pay for it. I said, "That must have been a whole week's pay!" His eyes got wide and he exclaimed, "A WEEK!!! Man, that was almost a month's pay!" He quickly and boldly wrote some nasty letters, one to each of the senators from Georgia, Senator Russell and Senator George, and one to his Representative.

He was promptly ordered to report to the tent of the mail censor who told him he shouldn't send those letters. All outgoing mail was read by censors before being sent to its destination. This was to assure that no unauthorized information would be revealed in case the mail fell into the hands of the enemy. If the page had writing on both sides, the censored words would be blacked out. Otherwise, the information in question would be *cut* out of the paper.

The censor could not stop Joe from sending the letters, but wanted to let him know that it could possibly get him into big trouble. Joe told him emphatically that he DID want those letters sent. To his pleasant surprise, in his very next pay check there was the reimbursement for the amount of $27. He laughed that the incident didn't win or lose the war, but it did show that somebody cared about those guys out there.

A beautiful end-of-the-story story must be told. The troop train Joe was on pulled into the terminal station in Atlanta en route to the mustering out center at Camp Lejeune. They had spent about seven days on the train crossing the country from California, so the troops were allowed to go out for calisthenics on the platform in the terminal while waiting for a short layover. The multi-storied twin buildings of the Southern Railway office complex overlooked the platform below. Some young ladies who worked in the offices were also overlooking the platform below, admiring what they saw from their windows. Suddenly there was a scream from one of the girls as she recognized Joe down there – it was his sister Reba. What a reunion that must have been for the two of them!

When Joe left for service, he was very much in love with a young lady who had gone to high school with him. They were not officially engaged, but they sort of had an understanding that they would wait for each other. While he was in Okinawa, he received a letter that began "Dear Joe." This immediately caught his attention since that was not the usual endearing salutation she normally used in her letters. She broke the news that she and a young man at home had decided to get married, so she would not be writing to him anymore. Such letters were called "Dear John" letters by the GIs.

Joe said he had never had anything in his life to hurt so much. It absolutely broke his heart. There he was, he said, fighting for his life and hers, not knowing if he would ever get back home or not, but planning to spend the rest of his life with her if he did. Then this.

Joe ends his story by telling me, "That was your sister Dot." So everything worked out alright after all. They have been married to each other since 1947.

PART FOUR

Back to Europe

❖ CHAPTER 8

The Quest

      After his retirement, Gene Cheatham's desire became stronger and stronger to go to Europe in search of the family that had been so attentive when his feet were frozen in combat in January, 1945. He had no idea where to begin this quest because he was not sure what town they were in at the time. He did know the date, however.

      He found a book that traced the action of the Third Armored Division throughout the war years, and through its pages, he determined that he was in a little town by the name of Lierneux, Belgium.

      As I have said earlier, Gene is my cousin but we were reared, his siblings and mine, as brothers and sisters. One day while Gene was playing golf with my own brother, Steve, the subject of Gene's dream of 50 years came up again. Steve had business connections in several parts of Europe and was very familiar with the territory, so he suggested that they go together and make this dream a reality.

      To begin, they contacted the Consulate General of Belgium in Atlanta, who then sent a letter to Belgium. The following are excerpts from that letter dated October 24, 1996:

"Dear Sir,

    <u>Re: American Liberation Army Veteran looking for the Belgian Family who saved his life</u>

      "I have been approached recently by a veteran of the American Liberation Army, Mr. Gene Cheatham. He told me the following story which you might find interesting.

"Mr. Cheatham was part of the Third Armored Division during the Battle of Ardennes[1] in 1945. Severely injured, he was (befriended) by a Belgian family in Lierneux, the night of the 6th to 7th January 1945. This family, risking the lives of its members, hid him and gave him medical help.

"Mr. Cheatham, who was in a state of shock, does not remember much and certainly not the name of that family, but he remembers that the family was living in a cellar in a railway station. The family consisted of the father and mother, a grandmother and two boys, about 9 and 11.

"As his feet were frozen, the family bathed them in warm water, a process completely forbidden by the American Army doctors. This process saved both feet from being amputated.

"Mr. Cheatham, who finally has the possibility to go to Belgium, would like to find the children of the Belgian family. He has decided to go to Lierneux where he is due to arrive on November 11.

"I thought that the story was worth telling. If you decide to publicise (sic) it in order to help that American citizen in his quest, may I suggest that those who have any information they could share, send their mail to the following address by diplomatic pouch and with a normal Belgian stamp........"

And publicize it, he did! Three newspapers and two television stations carried the story, and within 24 hours after the story broke, Gene received information about some members of the family. He was overjoyed.

---

[1] Ardennes is a region in NE France, NE Belgium, and Luxembourg. On a map, the front lines of battle made a bulging shape around this area. It was here that some of the bloodiest battles of WW II were fought. It became known as *The Battle of the Bulge,* beginning on December 16, 1944, and continuing for several weeks. Also, some WW I skirmishes took place here.

At city hall in Lierneux, a man burst into his secretary's office and told her to lay aside everything she was doing. He had an emergency that needed immediate attention. He gave her all the details he had learned from television and wanted her to get busy right away to find that family. It was already the end of October, and the news stories reported that he was due to arrive on November 11.

It seems like a fairy tale, but it so happened that the secretary lived right next door to the old railway station building which had been turned into a home for the elderly. Perhaps her boss was aware of that when he gave her the assignment, but I failed to get the facts on this.

She contacted an older woman she knew who had been living in the town during the war and asked for any information she might have. The woman had known the family and was happy to help. She recalled that their name was Laloux. They were living in the upper (third) floor of the building, but moved to the basement for safety when the shelling began. Furthermore, this woman had had a girlish 'crush' on one of the young boys and knew exactly where they were living in 1996!

Immediately, the following information was dispatched to Gene at his home in Acworth, Georgia:

"INFORMATION GIVEN BY Mrs. Monique Yunck, from the City Hall of Lierneux"
(Telephone numbers were given and her private address, to which was added, "Next to the old railway station.")
"INFORMATION RECEIVED: The parents are dead. Two sons are still living........*(giving names, addresses, and telephone numbers of the two men.)*"
"PRACTICAL INFORMATION:
"TRAIN – In Liege, take the train towards VIELSALM, step off in Vielsalm. There are hotels there, but none in Lierneux, distant (sic) of about 7 miles.
"TAXI – Once in Vielsalm if in need for a taxi, walk up the street in front of the railway station, towards the

main street. In that street, go to the LIBRAIRIE-AGENCE DE TAXIS. They will call a taxi for you.

"HOTEL – You will find hotels in Vielsalm, NONE in Lierneux.

"SPECIAL CEREMONY IN LIERNEUX ON MONDAY NOVEMBER 11, 1996 AT 10 AM: veterans of WW II will gather in Lierneux for a special ceremony. Mrs. Yunck recommends that you arrive on Sunday night in Vielsalm so as to be present the next day in Lierneux for the beginning of the ceremony. **HAVE A NICE TRIP"**

Gene related numerous memorable experiences during his visit which made him feel welcome. Everyone seemed happy to see him, and the people everywhere he went thanked him for what he had done for their country. Those people had suffered unbearably under the Third Reich, which was the Nazi regime beginning in 1933. They were liberated by the Allies when Germany surrendered in 1945, ending this terrible period under the dictatorship of Adolph Hitler.

As soon as Steve, Gene, and Gene's son Tony arrived in Belgium, they were greeted by a duchess who invited them to stay in her home during their visit. They declined the invitation, however, because they had already acquired a place to stay.

The ceremony for the Belgian veterans was held in an enormous church and was celebrating the anniversary of the armistice. When the men remarked about the large number of children in attendance, they were told that it was a requirement as part of their education so they would never forget that horrendous time in the history of their country.

Even though the ceremony was in French and could not be understood by the Americans, there seemed to be an electric presence in the room as each speaker took their place on the platform. One of the interpreters who had been assigned to the visitors also had a place on the program, and although Gene could recognize his own name spoken occasionally, he could not understand anything else.

The audience was attentive and perfectly quiet until the interpreter introduced Gene and asked him to stand. What happened when he got to his feet was awesome. He says he has never heard such an ovation, and it moved him deeply. What a pity we Americans are not as appreciative of what these men did for us. Germany and Japan had to be stopped, or our own country would have fallen under the rule of one or the other of them.

I asked him to tell me about his encounter with the Laloux sons, and he could only shake his head a moment before he could answer. "It was just wonderful," he said. "Like they were long lost relatives."

The two men, whose names are Joseph and Ferdinand, were found in Namur. One of them told Gene that the experience is still so vivid in his mind, he could even describe the pan with blue flowers on it that his mother used to bathe those huge feet.

It was learned that there was also a third son who had died in the early 1990s. At the time the Laloux family was caring for Gene, that son had been sent into hiding with a farm family because he was old enough to have been forced to serve in the German army, had he been found.

The wives of the three men told of the many times they had heard their husbands tell the story of the American soldier their mother cared for. Mme. Laloux often wondered, and again only shortly before her death, what might have happened to him. Oddly enough, she had also said at one time or another, "Who knows, one day he might just walk up and knock on our door."

Later, they were escorted to an old monastery and introduced to a man who was 12 years old when the Battle of the Ardennes ("The Bulge") took place. He was told that Gene had been in an American tank during the battle outside of Lierneux and had come back to visit the scene. The man insisted that there was no way any man could have survived inside a tank in that battle. Once he was convinced that he was actually looking at one who did, he threw his arms around Gene, became very emotional, and thanked him repeatedly. At 12 years old, he was old enough to remember, and to suffer, under Hitler's regime.

The entourage consisting of Gene, Steve, Tony, and three interpreters, one for each man, set out to locate the battlefield where this action took place. Some of the landscape looked familiar, and one mountain in particular seemed to be the place where thousands of German foot soldiers had been swarming over the mountainside.

They stopped at a farmhouse and explained their mission to an elderly woman who lived there. She pointed to an open field across the way and told them it had happened right across there. She added, "The air was so thick with bullets, it looked like swarms of bees." Exactly as it had been described earlier.

Gene has since made another trip to the area, taking his daughter Valerie with him the second time. They have become good friends with Monique, the lady at city hall in Lierneux who found the Laloux family, and she has visited her newfound friends here in the United States.

While visiting Monique, her father enjoyed telling them the story about being a prisoner of war. He was only nine years old when the Germans took over Belgium. One day some German soldiers asked the young boy for directions to Lierneux and he told them it had been moved and he didn't know where they took it. Because of his lack of respect and his sarcasm, he was taken to jail and locked up. He added that they kept him only about 30 minutes, but he can say he was a prisoner of war – at nine years old!

My conversation with Gene continued for several hours as he told me story after story about his trips to Europe, and about the friends he made while he was there who have visited him and his wife Betty in the United States. For instance, in one of his stories he told of trying to pay his escorts who took him throughout Belgium and Germany. They scolded him and was told he must never take his wallet out in their presence again because there is no way they could ever repay him for what he did for them and their country. In another incident, someone had arranged for him to be seated in the first class section of the plane for his trip home. When he arrived in the U.S., bright fluorescent PRIORITY stickers had been placed on his luggage, allowing him to avoid the hassle of going through customs.

I could go on and on recounting the stories and experiences he shared with me, but those would be a complete book of themselves. When we finished, I asked, "Do you think the people in our own country will ever learn to appreciate what you men did as much as those people do?" Emphatically, he answered, "Oh, no! The people in our country have not had to go through anything near to what those poor souls had to endure. There is no way a person can possibly relate to that kind of hell unless they have had to live through it."

Mr. and Mrs. Camille Laloux — 1945
Lierneux, Belgium

These photos were taken from an old snapshot.
Mme. Laloux and her family cared for Gene Cheatham
in Lierneux when his feet were severely frozen in
combat, January 1945.

The old railway building in Liemeux as it looked when Gene returned to Belgium in 1996. The Laloux family lived in the basement during the shelling of the town.

Gene and his son Tony overlooking the battlefield near Lierneux in 1996. The tree at the right of the photograph has been left standing because it is too riddled with metal from artillery fire for saws to be able to cut it down.

The 7th Sense

How can we remember
The ear shattering thunder of flak,
When this we have not heard?
How can we remember the searing heat of a bullet
When this we have not felt?
How can we remember
The blinding flashes of shell fire
When these we have not seen?
How can we remember
The sour-sweetness of our blood
as it trickled across our lips
When this we have not tasted?
How can we remember the thick, suffocating stench
Of smoke and decay,
When this we have not smelt?
We cannot.....
because we have been spared the Agony,
the Terror,
the Hellish sensations of War.....
.....by those who can.

This beautiful poem was written by a seventeen year old Belgian boy known only as Dennis. He sent it by a friend to Gene Cheatham's hotel room when he returned to Belgium in 1996 to find the family who had saved his life in 1945.

PART FIVE

Women's Role in Defense

❖ CHAPTER 9

Billie Rogers Caldwell

The Bell Bomber plant in Marietta, Georgia, made B-29 airplanes during the war. The *Enola Gay,* the name given to the plane that dropped the atomic bomb on Hiroshima, Japan, was a B-29 bomber. Hordes of workers traveled every day from miles around to work at the plant. One of those was a cousin of mine who lived in Rome, in the northwest part of the state. She rode an hour or so, one way, to and from work.

Billie Rogers (later Mrs. C. M. Caldwell) was only 20 or 21 when she applied for a job there. It was a high security job, as you might well know, so she had to be fingerprinted, have a birth certificate, and all sorts of things that were not usually as strictly checked then as they are nowadays.

She was hired and placed in the cable department, located on the mezzanine right next to the radio department.

Radar was in its infancy in the early 1940s, and the technology was proving to be an invaluable device in detecting the enemy. Foreign powers would go to any lengths to get their hands on it, and the United States would go to any lengths to protect it. When placing the radar equipment in the B-29s, its location was periodically changed to different areas inside the aircraft. This was for security reasons, in case a plane fell into enemy hands. 'Travelers' in the factory went from department to department making the changes. In flight, a designated crew member on the plane was assigned the responsibility of destroying the vital equipment, if necessary.

Since only spliced cable held the coveted radar in place on the B-29s, processing the remaining cables was an exacting job. The cables Billie worked with had to be tested on a "proof-loader" machine to determine how much tension they could withstand. Not only was it exacting, but it was also potentially dangerous. Should one of the cables snap, it could easily slash a body in two.

On one occasion, a co-worker cut his cables a little too short and wanted Billie and her girl friend, who worked with her on the machine, to stretch them beyond a safe limit. The girls refused to do it. They caught a lot of flack from some of the less scrupulous workers because of it, but they were certain they had done the right thing. Billie's defense was that his defective cables could cost someone his life.

Billie worked nine hours a day, and adding the long ride, it made for an exhausting day. She said she was a sleepy head and would sometimes snooze on her way to work – and *always* on her way home!

She lived with her older sister and family for a while in Acworth, and rode with her sister's husband who also worked at the plant. That cut off a few miles for her. At one time she car-pooled with some other workers. That must have been a risky thing to do since gasoline and tires were so difficult to get. However, provisions could be made through the ration board to allow extra gasoline for defense workers and a few other occupations requiring the use of a vehicle. She told me a story about an incident that could have resulted in a tragedy. Tires were so scarce they were not even available most of the time, regardless of whether or not a car owner could get a ration stamp to purchase them. EVERYBODY drove on 'bald' tires.

On the road to work one day, another car passed the car she was riding in and made distressing motions at their tires. Her driver stopped to see what the trouble was and spotted a huge bulge on one of the tires. Before he could stoop down to examine it, the tire exploded and temporarily deafened him. When I remarked that they could have wrecked when it blew out if they had not been stopped, Billie laughed and said nobody could drive fast enough for that.

Perhaps it was incidences like that one that prompted the Smokey Mountain Trailways Bus Company to begin routes throughout the area for the workers at Bell Bomber. Buses ran regularly to Canton, Ellijay, Blue Ridge, and vicinities, on schedules that allowed each shift to get to their jobs on time.

Her tire story reminded me of a time that a car full of us teenagers were allowed to go into town. We lived a few miles out in the country and, since boredom had set in from not being able to go anywhere, we were absolutely elated one day when we were allowed to have the car keys. We were warned that we could go to the movies and nowhere else because there was very little gas in the car and no more was available. Well, if you know anything at all about young teenagers, a car, and the car keys, you know very well that this particular automobile on that particular day did not go straight to the movies and back home. Patriotism was not even a consideration with car keys in hand. The other teenagers in town just MUST see us out joy-riding!

Well, we lived in the north Georgia mountains, so we turned off the ignition and coasted down every hill to conserve gasoline. Little did we know it took more to crank it back up again. But to top that, *we had FOUR flat tires before we got back home!* The old inner tubes were so patched we bumped along the road like a pogo stick.

Back to Billie's story:

She told me of a tragic thing that happened on her shift one day. It was not in her department, so she did not see it, but the entire plant was affected by it.

There was a department where a tool called a drop hammer was used. Exactly as the name implies, a very large, heavy hammer dropped with great force to mold or join certain airplane parts. It was an extremely dangerous operation and required the operator's undivided attention.

One day a young man looked away from his work for a split second and the hammer came down on him and crushed his head. It will never be known how many workers in our defense plants might have lost their lives during the war years. They, too, did it for their country. She added that very few accidents occurred in the plant because extreme safety measures and precautions were emphasized regularly.

Battey General Hospital was built in Rome by the government to accommodate some of the wounded servicemen. Radio stations in the city urged the citizens of Rome to invite these men into their homes for a good meal, or just for a visit. Many of them were able to leave the hospital for a few hours, even though they were not well enough to be dismissed. This helped to pass the long days and weeks, and possibly helped to relieve their homesickness.

Billie's mother (my aunt) asked her family what they thought of that. Should she invite one of the servicemen to dinner? Her husband (who was my Uncle John), Billie, and her little sister Carolyn who is several years younger, thought it would be a good idea. Then Uncle John, in his typical dry wit, said he thought she should invite a soldier for Billie, and they could invite a Boy Scout for Carolyn.

This story, the same as those of the other civilians I have included in these biographies, clearly shows how the people at home united in an effort to win that awful war. Without the willingness of every citizen to contribute a part, however small or large, the end of the story might have been different. As Billie put it in my interview with her, everybody was everybody's brother, all willing to help each other and endure a measure of inconvenience to bring our boys back home.

❖ CHAPTER 10

Mary Siniard Cheatham

I knew that Mary Siniard was one of the thousands upon thousands of women who took over jobs vacated by the men who were being called into military service. These women contributed immeasurably to the war effort. Mary later married Bill Cheatham, making her a part of the family of whom I am so proud. I asked her to tell her story.

Mary was a young lady working in her hometown of Cartersville, Georgia, when it was announced that recruiters would be in town looking for anyone willing to work in a defense plant. She and several of her friends decided to attend the meeting to see what it was all about.

The Naval Ordinance Plant in Macon made ammunition for the war, so the job would not be as safe as her current job, but five girl friends decided to go anyway.

They went together on a bus and directly to the employment office in Macon as they had been instructed to do by the recruiter. They were told that someone from the Naval Ordinance Plant would pick them up there and take them to a place to stay for the night. Tired as they were, it was after 9 o'clock before security guards came for them.

The people of Macon opened up their homes to those who were coming to work in the plant, and also to the wives of soldiers stationed in the four military camps in the area. Anyone who had a spare room was willing to rent it to the influx of civilians pouring into the city. In this way, everyone was contributing in some way to the war effort.

The girls were taken to a home for the night, but it quickly proved that it would not work out for them to stay indefinitely. The room had only two beds, so two slept in one bed and three in the other. Not long after they bedded down for the night, one of the beds broke, so it was a pretty miserable night for five tired young girls, some who were away from home for the first time in their lives.

The girls were to have two weeks of training at the vocational school before beginning work. The next morning they were transported to the school and told not to leave because another place would be found for them to sleep, and transportation would be provided. Workers were desperately needed at the plant, so the recruits were treated well and were made as comfortable and safe as possible.

Again, it was about 9 o'clock before security guards from the plant took the girls to the place provided for them. It was a lovely home owned by a pharmacist, and they were very comfortable there, even though all five of them were in one room. The large home had three other rooms which were occupied by wives of soldiers. It is hard to imagine so many females living under one roof and enjoying it.

Mary laughs about going into town one Sunday afternoon not long after they moved to Macon. She says she has no idea *why,* but all five of the girls decided to dress in white. The streets were teeming with soldiers, and wherever they went, the guys called them "the nurses." It was a fun time, even in the worst of times.

If the girls went home on weekends, they traveled by bus. Usually, it was so crowded there would be no seats available and the aisles were full of people standing. Almost everyone traveled by bus or train during that time because gasoline and tires were rationed, if available at all. Macon to Atlanta was a grueling trip, standing on a swaying Greyhound bus wheeling down old Highway 41. Mary added that no one ever seemed to complain. It was just something that had to be done. It was a time for everyone to contribute to the war effort, however small.

Mary lived in the pharmacist's home for about nine months. Her two brothers were drafted, leaving their mother with no one to care for her, so Mary went back to Cartersville.

Three of the other girls stayed for two and a half years, until the end of the war. They had gone home for a few days vacation, and while there the war ended and the plant closed immediately.

I questioned Mary about the working conditions, and just what her job entailed. She said they worked in small cubicles, surrounded by steel walls and doors to protect other parts of the building in case of an explosion. She mostly worked with small ammunition, filling the shells with pellets.

Mary's husband, Bill, told me of an incident that happened to her while she worked at the plant. He thought it was humorous, but Mary didn't think it was so funny.

The workers had been warned not to drop a shell, or allow one to roll off the table. One day while she and another girl were working in their cubicle, a shell rolled onto the floor. Both girls made a lightning-fast exit through the door leading to the outside. Their supervisor happened by just at that time and asked where they were. Someone pointed out the door to two scared girls who were many, many yards across a field by this time – and still running.

I commented on the fact that she was to be commended because she had put her life in jeopardy to work in such a place. Mary very modestly says that she did what she could for the war effort, never thinking twice about it. Somebody had to do it because our men were gone and there was no one else. What she did was just a small contribution.

I corrected her by saying it was no "small" contribution. I feel that people should know about the contributions she, and other women like her, made on behalf of our country. They played such an important part in winning that war. Our nation was short of manpower, having just come out of World War I not a generation before. Without the spunk of the women of this country back on the home front, we can only wonder what the outcome might have been – and shiver at the thought of what it *would* have been.

PART SIX

Civilians' Role in Defense

❖ CHAPTER 11

Student Interview No. 1

Every year when my classes studied the unit on World War I and World War II in their history book, the students were given the assignment to interview someone who was living during World War II and give a report in class. The following report contained information different from any of the others, and I asked for a copy. Here it is, just as the grandmother of one of my former students wrote it in her own words.

"No one could believe the Pearl Harbor news when it came on that fateful Sunday. Some said later that it was not altogether such a surprise to certain people involved in government, but to the average citizen it came almost as 'the end of the world.'

"It soon became apparent that everyone had to do his part – men, who could, to the service or war plants, and women to war plants and to take over the home fronts. My husband volunteered but was not accepted because of asthma.

"Naturally as the war continued there were shortages. We had stamp books for products such as coffee, sugar, meat, gas -- almost everything we had come to think of as necessities quickly became treats. Even with stamps one could not always buy because the stores didn't always have the products in house. I think that most of all I missed bacon. I was raised having a complete breakfast which included grits, biscuits, bacon, oatmeal and coffee. My mother said breakfast, a <u>balanced</u> meal, gave you more mind-power for the day ahead. If we had bacon every three weeks during war time we were lucky and knew how to be thankful for it. In fact, with all the hardships, I believe people –

American people – who were used to having so much, really for the first time knew how to truly <u>be</u> thankful.

"It was a time, too, for people to come together – work together – for the common good for this country and each other.

"I was employed at (a bank) at the time. When rationing started, stamps given to stores for products had to be deposited at the bank by the store owner. Each merchant had to open an account for each rationed product he sold. It was my job at the bank to oversee all rationing accounts. This included accepting the stamps the same way as accepting money in regular accounts. A grocer, for instance, would have a sugar account, a bacon account, a coffee account, etc. The overall name of the account, for instance would be The Rogers Store with all the various foods in separate accounts under the Rogers name. The stamps were pasted to large sheets holding 100 stamps, each stamp representing 5 lbs. of sugar for instance. It was rather easy to count as I took the deposit. The store owner would give checks, similar to money checks, to his wholesale dealer for the products rationed to him. It was my duty at the end of each day to put each stamp sheet under an ultra violet light to determine if they were real or counterfeit. Each sheet had to be stamped by the depositor for an endorsement so I could determine which store had given me counterfeit stamps. That depositor was called and told he had to make the stamps good – his account was debited for the amount. If he did not make them good I had to notify the federal government and a case would be made against the store owner in federal court. You might be surprised how many times I had to go to federal court in Valdosta, Ga. – the nearest federal court – to testify against store owners who weren't careful enough when they accepted them from their customers. This didn't make me too popular to say the least. Too bad that anyone would not have the 'good of the country' in mind instead of making a 'fast buck' off of a tempting situation.[2]

---

[2] There were, sadly enough, people who were not willing to be inconvenienced and, if they could find a merchant greedy enough to risk selling something without a stamp – and if the buyer had enough money to pay the asking price – many goods were bought and sold on the black market.

"The war was a time for staying glued to your radio all day long at work or at home to get the latest news about the 'front lines' and the local news about those killed, wounded, or lost in action. I had a brother who happened to be on the *USS St. Paul,* the ship which fired the last shot in the war from her barrels. He came home unhurt luckily, but died the first night home with heart failure. Also a classmate of mine was killed, and a 'first sweetheart' who was held prisoner of war for years before he got to come home. The military car that brought service personnel to the front door to inform a family of deaths, injured, or lost, was the most dreaded sight at the home places.

"I can't say that my family suffered unduly – we just did without things mostly – but suffered no real hardships. However, in 1945 our house burned and the only way we could build back was to scour the countryside buying a few pieces wherever we could find anything available in house construction. The builders would work each day with whatever we had for them or go home early. When we finally did complete our home, we couldn't find a cook stove nor refrigerator – we used an old icebox we put chunks of ice in every other day and bought a two-burner electric unit (no oven) which we used for two years.

"I suppose you can never say there's an advantage to war – how horrible the thought – but there are certainly lessons to be learned living through one. Too bad each generation has to learn it over again. There is, however, a togetherness regardless of rich, poor, race or stature among all people on 'your' side in your hometown, your state, nation and even with friendly nations overseas that you don't always feel without a war to make bond of 'all for one and one for all.'

"In thinking about the war years, I recall the wonderful music that came out of suffering, death, loneliness, sorrow, comradeship, love and kindness – Don't Sit Under the Apple Tree with Anyone Else but Me; Boogie Woogie Bugle Boy; I'll Be with You in Apple Blossom Time; I Left My Heart at the Stage Door Canteen; Coming In on a Wing and A Prayer – all Grammy award potentials by the Andrew Sisters. Listen to these songs if you have opportunity. The words make sense and will thrill your being.

"As you study and learn more about our national conflicts, perhaps it will encourage you to remember the courageous people who defended our country through all the years and when someone says 'Veteran's Day' you will give thanks to the people who maintained 'our way' of freedom for your generation, and you will help to take up the challenge with strength, love, and duty."

The stamps, or coupons, mentioned in these interviews did not *purchase* the item, as we know 'food stamps' today. It was a means of dividing (or rationing) goods among the civilians. Each person could have only a certain portion within a certain time, and a stamp must be presented at the time of purchase to prove the right to buy it. Each family member had a book with his name on it. Canned goods were difficult to find since all metals went into the war effort. Many other items were hard to get. Anything shipped from another country, such as coffee, tea, or sugar could not get to the U.S. because the shipping lanes on the high seas were endangered. Leather for boots, rubber for tires, or any petroleum products went to the military, so civilians had little or nothing made from those products.

❖ CHAPTER 12

Student Interview No. 2

Another interesting report came from a young student who got so caught up in his assignment of the war years that he made a long distance call to his grandfather in New Jersey. He put the telephone receiver to his tape recorder, then wrote the following words from the tape to share the interview with his classmates. The memories of his grandfather brought back memories of my own. This is his account as the student transcribed it from his recorded conversation.

"The earliest I can remember of World War II was when I was ten years old. It was early in the morning on a Sunday. I was walking down the street when people began to come out of houses. They were yelling and crying and saying that Pearl Harbor was bombed. I remember I was worried because I had an older brother that was stationed at Pearl Harbor. Later we found out he was okay.

"Everyone was suppose to help in the war effort even the children. At our school we collected rubber tires, rags, tin foil[3],

----

[3] What we now call aluminum foil was known as 'tin foil.' Chewing gum and cigarettes were wrapped in paper that was laminated on one side with a thin layer of tin foil. Children would collect these wrappers, peal off that tiny amount of foil, and roll it into a ball. Piece after piece was added to the ball until it would be as large as a baseball, or larger. We had contests to see who could have the largest ball of foil on the day we turned in all of our 'collectibles.'

and scraps of any kind of metal. Everything changed for us children. I can remember I had a pack of cards like baseball cards but instead of the player there were pictures of enemy airplanes. This was so that the children could identify the planes if one flew over.

"At night we had air raid drills or all lights out. During these drills we had to either turn the lights out or hang black cloths over the windows. My father was an air raid warden. It was his job to make sure everyone in our neighborhood had their lights out. If you were driving a car at night and there was a drill, you had to shut off the lights and stop the car wherever you were. As far as I know there was never any enemy planes spotted. These were only drills.

"In 1943 a German submarine was captured in Perth Amboy, New Jersey, by the Coast Guard. This was close to where I lived so we went down to look at it.

"I remember the letters my mother use to get from my older brothers that were in the war. Sometimes there were words blacked out. Sometimes cut out. This was called censoring. Anything that the war department thought could be a threat in the hands of the enemy like times, shipments, or locations, were taken out. My brother Bob was wounded in the war. He was shot in the leg with a German wooden bullet.[4] He is still alive.

"My grandmother worked at the Raritan Arsenal in Raritan, New Jersey where she made bullets and guns. A lot of the women had to work in war factories.

"Things were done differently at this time like the coupons you had to have in order to buy gas or sugar or meat.

"The music was about boy friends or husbands away at war. The most popular dance was the jitter-bug."

---

[4] The Germans sometimes used wooden bullets in order only to wound our troops rather than to kill them. They knew that when an American soldier was *killed,* his rifle was stood in the dirt beside the body, which was then left to be retrieved later, hardly slowing down the other men. However, when a man was only *wounded,* his comrades would not leave him there unattended. To carry him for medical help would require two or three other GIs, not only slowing down our troops, but also taking more of them out of combat.

PART SEVEN

A Little Sentimental

❖ CHAPTER 13

My Own Father – World War I

      In the very beginning words of this book, I emphasized the fact that the stories recorded here would be about only those men and women I could interview personally. This was so that I could be absolutely sure the information was accurate. It is obvious that this story about my father would not have come from a personal interview.

      I am most fortunate to have in my possession some letters written by my dad to his folks back home in 1918 and 1919. Since they are written in his own handwriting, dated, and postmarked, I have no doubt that this story, too, is accurate. At any rate, I have decided to include some excerpts from some of his letters. I got a great amount of pleasure in reading through them, and a bit of sadness, too. It made me realize how much I missed, not having him during my growing up years.

      Oliver Stephen Lackey was an infantryman in The Great War, or World War I, as we know it today. It was thought to be "the war to end all wars" because there was a tremendous amount of new technology that contributed to making it more terrible than any previous war. Machine guns, tanks, and airplanes were used in warfare for the first time. The airplane had been invented only a few years. Man's first flight in the Kitty Hawk was in 1903, and the war began in 1914. The airplane was less than a dozen years old!

      Although there is not much history to glean from these letters, I learned a lot about my father as a person. I learned that he could make the best of what he had been dealt, and he could find humor even on the battlefield – just as the other men whose stories are told here.

In one letter he wrote, "We are in a noisy place, but we don't mind it much now any more than those trains running." (He was a railroad man.) That was dated September 23, 1918.

On October 24, 1918 he wrote. "I have seen places I could enjoy visiting much better than the trenches but our co. held their own and all came back. I read your letter in 65 yds of the Germans, that is close enough isn't it, but we are enroute to Berlin and can't be stopped."

He was a victim of the poisonous gas used by the Germans during that war, and was hospitalized just before the Armistice was signed. I had been told that he was gassed on Armistice day, November 11, 1918, but from things he says in some of these letters, I believe that information was incorrect, and it happened sometime before that date.

On January 8, 1919, he wrote home on American Red Cross stationery. At the top he has written "Pvt. O.S. Lackey, Base Hospital #93, Room #166, Cannes, France." Then he says, "I am at present living the life of Riley. We landed here last Sunday the 5th and we are getting the very best of care and this is the most beautiful place I have ever seen.............

"French girls are real nice and good looking and sweet as can be but I can't explain my feelings when I first heard the voice of a real American woman but I can remember very distinctly where and when it was and how it came about. There were two or three of us together and I said bon zhoor madam moselle *(perhaps he could speak French better than he could spell it!)* and she replied good morning boys. We stopped to see if she was a real American or just a French woman who could speak English real good. The next time I heard an American lady's voice was as they rolled me off the litter on to a cot one said how do you feel soldier but I had to wait for a minute or so to answer as my feeling was changing rapidly."

January 14, 1919, Cannes, France: ".........I thought for a while I was going to push daisies for the Frenchmen but I escaped the job. I think I am alright now though as I feel good and I am back to my weight. I think if I stay here long at Cannes I will get to 200."

I don't know when he was able to be brought back to the States, but I have a letter dated April 6, 1919. It is also on Red Cross stationery from U.S. Debarkation Hospital No. 3, Sixth Ave. and 18th St., New York City. He writes, ".......You need not worry about what has happened to me for I have gone through showers of shrapnel and machine gun bullets and never got a scratch. My ailments are just a little gas, pneumonia, and influenza, so I'll be fine."

Oliver Stephen Lackey met Nellie Bennett after he was discharged from the Army. They were married in June, 1920, and after visiting some Western states on their honeymoon, lived in Birmingham, Alabama, for several years. He worked in the Southern Railway offices there, but was later transferred to Atlanta in the freight rate department.

My mother, Nell, lost a long battle with cancer on February 2, 1941, at the age of 46. My father died four months later on June 7, 1941, due to complications from ruptured appendix. He was 48. There were five of us children ranging in age from two years old to 19.

Now I'm back to where I began..........His sister, Maude, took four of us into her home and treated us like her very own. Our oldest sister, Mary Nell, was already out of school and was a career girl, so she stayed in Atlanta.

If your family has stories to tell, I strongly urge you to listen to them and, if possible, write them down. You will be glad you did.

(See pictures on next page ⇨)

Pvt. Oliver Stephen Lackey - 1918

My own father in his doughboy uniform in
World War I.   Infantrymen were called
doughboys, although I have no idea why.

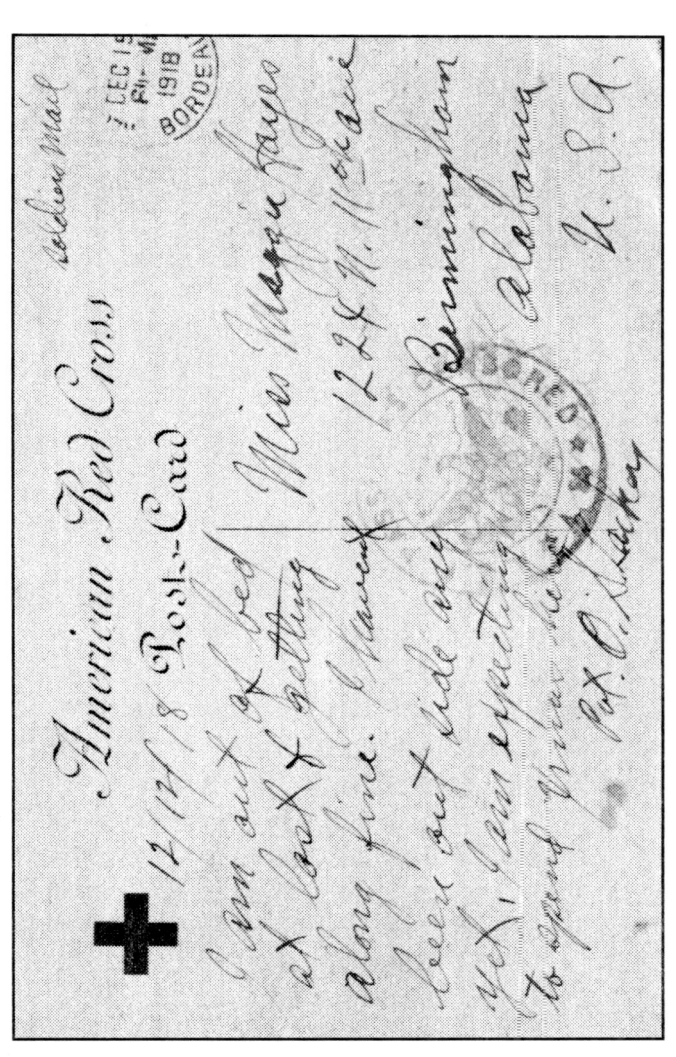

A post card to his cousin dated December 12. 1918.